OFF THE AIR

Off the Air:
Thoughts About Our Quality of Life

By Terry Phillips

Hye Books
Bakersfield, California
www.HyeBooks.com

For information, please contact Hye Books, P.O. Box 12492, Bakersfield, CA 93389.

ISBN 978-1-892918-04-8

Cover design by Don Howe

Microphone image courtesy of Wes Dooley, Audio Engineering Associates

Table of Contents

Right and Wrong

Troubling Trend in Public Radio News

Pass it on…

Dedication

This book is dedicated to freedom of expression.

"All human beings are born free and equal in dignity and rights. They are endowed with reason and conscience and should act towards one another in a spirit of brotherhood."
-United Nations Universal Declaration of Human Rights, Article I

"Congress shall make no law respecting an establishment of religion, or prohibiting the free exercise thereof; or abridging the freedom of speech, or of the press; or the right of the people peaceably to assemble, and to petition the Government for a redress of grievances."
-United States Constitution, Bill of Rights, First Amendment

Foreword
By Jim Meyers

Choosing Terry Phillips to be the new host of "Quality of Life" was one of those easy decisions that come along from time to time. Mr. Phillips' credentials and his international journalistic experience were important considerations, but his interest in moderating well-informed discussions in a civil manner, while adhering to strict ethical standards was the deciding factor.

For about 57 minutes each week, Terry drew opinions and facts from his guests and callers, then for a minute or two would give us his commentary on the issue of the day. You will find a common thread in Terry's commentaries: a call to be reasonable, civil, respectful and to improve the manner in which we handle social conflict.

In these commentaries you will find an appreciation for good advice from sources such as H.L. Mencken: "There is always an easy solution to every human problem. Neat, plausible and wrong." You'll find observations like this one from George Carlin: "A lot of the people who worry about the safety of nuclear power plants don't bother wearing seat belts." You will find an appreciation of theater, not just as art or entertainment, but also in asserting the importance of freedom, to give voice to political and social ideas. He reminds us, for example, that for decades, the U.S. Government banned the anti-war play "Lysistrata." The play was written by Aristophanes more than 2400 years ago. The same play was banned in 1967 by the military junta, ironically, in Greece.

I don't want to spoil the fun, but do check out Terry's idea for selecting a U.S. President in commentary #72.

Terry Phillips is a hard-working, ethical journalist with something to say. His commentaries from "Quality of Life" are a nice way to get to know him.

???

Note: For many years, Jim Meyers was program director and station manager at Valley Public Radio. He retired in 2010.

Introduction

California's heartland is a microcosm of the United States. In this region live Americans of all stripes: conservatives, moderates and liberals; religious and secular; new immigrants who speak several languages and those with long roots who speak only one; highly-educated business executives; industrial and agricultural laborers.

They all have one thing in common: this place.

Fresno is the largest city in the Central Valley and home to a public radio station where, for more than five years, I moderated a weekly interview/call-in program called "Quality of Life" -- hence, the subtitle of this book.

"Quality of Life" re-defined talk radio in Central California. Beyond the chaotic insanity of insults and incivility that dominate the airwaves, we provided a haven for refreshing, grown-up conversation.

This one-hour weekly program was an honest and open-minded forum. It covered politics, world affairs, health care, entertainment, education, business, agriculture, philosophy, and more. Expert guests came from all points of view. Listener participation -- a significant portion of most programs -- was often provocative but always polite. The voices were bi-partisan, non-partisan, post-partisan, middle of the road -- even off the road.

There were no hidden agendas. No yelling and screaming. No kidding. Well, maybe a little kidding. We tried not to take ourselves too seriously.

Our broadcast brought together expert guests and listeners from myriad points of view. We provided a bias-free forum for everyone who was reasonable and respectful. It was, by all accounts, a very successful (albeit rare) exercise in polite public discourse on the air.

Agriculture was a popular topic, beginning with our very first program. In addition to being California's breadbasket, the Central Valley had become the state's fastest growing region. An increase in population was exerting pressures on such limited resources as land and water.

The single most frequent topic on "Quality of Life" was health. We talked about many issues -- from the causes and possible cures for various illnesses, to advances in medical technology. We also discussed the politics of health insurance.

One regular feature of this program was a personal commentary (or, if you will, "CommenTerry"). Sometimes, it was related to the hour's topic; other times, not. Over the years, I was asked to provide listeners a transcript of these essays. From time to time, friends suggested publishing a compilation of them. This seems an appropriate moment to do so.

Language purists should note that I wrote these radio scripts to be heard, not seen on the printed page. That is my explanation for any errors of style or grammar.

My relationship with Valley Public Radio ended in early 2011. After a dispute over creative control, I wrote an op-ed piece critical of funders attempting to influence content. That essay ("Troubling Trend in Public Radio News") was published in *The Fresno Bee* on Feb. 11, 2011.

A few days later, the station's general manager called to inform me that I was no longer the host for "Quality of Life" and turned over the reins of my show to the new program director. If not for this conflict, I would happily have continued producing and moderating the program.

Instead, I return to my first and constant profession, that of traveler. Wherever the road takes me, I hope our paths will cross again someday. Until then, dear reader, I close as always with this reminder: It's not only the QUANTITY that counts. It's the QUALITY of life.

-Terry Phillips

FOOD AND DRINK

1: Agriculture
June 19, 2007

Raising crops has always been hard work. Even with modern technology, living off the land is, you should pardon the expression, a dirty job. Without farmers to cultivate that dirt, we might as well go back to the jungle, because the soil nourishes us all.

On the other hand, as our world continues to shrink and barriers to trade continue to drop, we find ourselves dealing with a different kind of jungle -- the jungle of unregulated capitalism.

As Americans, the word "freedom" is at the very core of our national philosophy. We believe in freedom of speech, freedom of religion, freedom of assembly, and most importantly, the freedom to do business. You've probably heard that cynical turn on the golden rule, "He who has the gold makes the rules." But when money becomes the only commodity, all of us become expendable.

At some point, someone needs to stand up and say, "Wait a minute. Unlimited freedom is not good for us."

We need farmers for our very survival. We should be at least as concerned about them disappearing as we are about other endangered species. We must protect local agriculture from the vicissitudes of land value and currency exchange rates.

The marketplace alone should not determine the fate of our food. The pressures of globalization and urbanization make it harder than ever for farmers to afford working the land rather than selling it.

Of course, everyone is free to buy and sell, whether it's the crops they grow or the land itself. But there should be some reasonable limitations on the trade of both. And that works both ways. We should be neither victims of globalization, nor planetary predators. Fellow farmers in other places deserve respect, too. This goes back to the good old golden rule -- the real golden rule. We must treat others the way we wish to be treated, friend and foe alike, because it's a small world.

2: Obesity
November 20, 2007

I find it ironic that poor people are often overweight and undernourished. There was a time when girth was a measure of success. But as our diet has deteriorated from a largely natural one to extremely artificial, we can eat badly and still weigh a lot.

On one hand, if (as some say) less is more, you could argue that least is most. It is, after all, unhealthy to eat more than we need. On the other hand, it's not just the quantity that counts. I sometimes wonder how much better life would be with less -- less food, less stuff, less junk.

That is definitely true when it comes to knickknacks. Now, I'm sure my mother and sister are laughing as they hear me say this, knowing how much of a packrat I am. I really like stuff. Still, there is also a certain burden to possessions. Things need to be stored, secured, maintained, and occasionally, replaced.

Of course, it's easy to envy the wealthy. They do have more stuff than the rest of us. The also eat more. They eat better, too. Then again, some rich people are fat. But that's little consolation. Because when it comes to food, or housing or anything else, the concentration of ownership worldwide leaves relatively few very well-fed and the majority hungering for more.

By the way, that is true for the media we consume, as well. I hope you're aware the FCC is trying to relax cross-ownership rules for print and broadcast. That topic deserves our full attention and I hope we'll talk about it in the coming weeks.

Meanwhile, I'm trying to cut down on some of my stuff, both inside and out. I encourage you to do the same and consider sharing your surplus with others less fortunate.

3: Controlled Substances
July 29, 2008

Central Valley vineyards produce some excellent wines. When consumed in moderation, fine wine tastes good. It can enhance food, and it is generally believed to be beneficial for our health.

I wondered whether anyone would call to point out the dangers associated with alcoholic beverages. Excess drinking can cause ailments ranging from loss of motor functions to cirrhosis of the liver and even death. Some people are especially susceptible to alcohol. For them, even a little bit can be too much.

Intoxication is a strange phenomenon. Most of us enjoy being a little tipsy from time to time. Even as children, we spin ourselves to the point of dizziness because, well, because it's fun. But grown-ups consider it unseemly to whirl around on the front lawn in order to get high. So instead, we drink or inhale or snort or inject. Some substances are socially acceptable and legally sanctioned. Others are not.

Some religions condemn such altered states. But in the last century, we learned that government prohibition doesn't work. Nevertheless, federal law continues to ban some causes of insobriety -- marijuana, cocaine, heroin -- the list is too long to read. It's easier to cite the legal drugs: alcohol, tobacco and caffeine.

The rationale for banning all the others has always been to protect the public health. But we know the real reason. Booze, cigarettes, coffee and tea are big business. These industries don't want competition from something you can grow in your backyard or brew in your bathtub or cook in your garage.

Now, I'm not suggesting that we legalize methamphetamines. Nor do I think we should permit children to abuse their growing bodies with drugs. On the other hand, isn't it about time that our government stopped intruding in the private lives of adults?

What difference should it make to me whether my next door neighbor has a glass of cabernet sauvignon with his steak or rolls a joint as part of a strictly vegetarian diet? I'd like to believe my tax dollars could be put to better use than enforcing some archaic myths about reefer madness. Shouldn't we worry more about the long-term effects of intoxicants on those who would be President? If athletes have to take tests for drug use, maybe politicians should, too.

November 11, 2008

William Saroyan wrote most impressively about the quality of life in his hometown. The way he described Fresno, it could have been almost anyone's hometown, more a state of mind than anything else.

My own childhood memories here include backyard vegetable gardens and fruit trees. We descendants of immigrants retain a certain attachment to the soil and an instinct for self-reliance. That means growing our own food from time to time.

Nothing beats the taste of a freshly picked apricot, ripe on the tree. Not to mention that it's a lot cheaper than paying three or four or five bucks a pound in a supermarket. Well, I guess corporations need to turn a profit, too. It's the American way. Or is it?

I worry about this country. Have we gone so far from the vision of our pioneering predecessors that we're now living the life they fought to flee? Forget taxation without representation. How about powerful people in some far off land deciding what we must pay for everything? It seems downright un-American!

I am shocked whenever I discover yet another home-grown product that is imported. Apricots from Turkey. Turkeys from Toronto. What's next: grapes from China?

It seems to me that we are becoming increasingly dependent on others for all our goods. I believe it is vital for each of us to produce something for ourselves. The easiest thing to begin with food. Plant a potato. Cultivate a crop of carrots. Pick a peck of pickled peppers for Pete's sake.

As you might have heard on this radio station over the weekend, we Americans grew much of our own food during World War II in the form of victory gardens. First lady Eleanor Roosevelt even planted one in front of White House. Replacing lawns with family gardens today not only makes good economic sense. That sort of land use is also smart agricultural policy. Who knows? Before long, we might bring more farming to the Central Valley and all live the American dream again.

February 3, 2009

I often try to find some humor in the topics we discuss on this radio program. Well, not today. Brace yourself for some cold, hard, humorless facts.

According to the UN World Food Program, twenty-five thousand people die of hunger every day. That's one person every three seconds.

In the United States, one out of every eight children goes to bed hungry. According to the US Census Bureau, twenty percent of Central Valley residents do not have enough to eat. Ironically, we throw away more than $100 million worth of food in America every day.

Now, let's put things in proper perspective. I said that one in eight American children goes to bed hungry. That means seven out of eight are not hungry. Twenty percent of Central Valley residents live in poverty. That means eighty percent are not poor.

So, which is it? Are we in trouble or not? Like most people, I used to think of hunger as a third-world problem, something that happened to somebody, somewhere else. It's not. Hunger is a human problem.

Any person who does not have enough food to eat, no matter where he or she lives, is hungry. That's not a statistic. That is the condition of our species. Of course, when a tragedy like hunger befalls you or a member of your family or a close friend, you tend to take it personally. When it happens to some stranger, well, that's just too bad.

Let me leave you with this (you should pardon the expression) food for thought. Last night, I had a very fulfilling dinner at a nice restaurant here in town with a friend of mine. The meal was delicious. We didn't have to wait long to be served and I didn't even have to pay. My friend treated me.

Nearly one billion members of our human family are hungry. This is the twenty-first century. I think they've waited long enough. Don't you? Let's feed them. We can figure out who will pick up the tab later.

6: Animal Cruelty
February 10, 2009

I have great sympathy for the way farm animals are treated. Most of us don't think about whether cattle or poultry are comfortable before they're slaughtered and eaten. I suppose we have a mental barrier between living creatures and food. Not having grown up on a farm, I'm not sure how easy it would be for me to kill a chicken or a cow -- even if I were very hungry.

The humane treatment of other species is not put on the same level as humans. If it were, I guess we'd all have to be vegans or at least vegetarians. But we're not. Most of us do eat meat. My Big Fat Greek Wedding aside, that includes lamb.

And what is human life worth? We were supposed to be created equal. But does an American have the same value as a non-American? Is a convict on death row treated the same as a member of Congress? Many people use the word "sacred" to describe life. That's one reason we have such passionate differences over birth control, capital punishment and assisted suicide. I hope to take up those issues on this program in the weeks to come.

Meanwhile, I leave you with this: In August 2003, Wired magazine published an article setting the sum total value of our body parts at about seventeen bucks. But if you take into consideration all the possible fluids, tissues and organs that can be extracted, the figure goes up to more than $46 million. Seems like most of us are vastly underpaid.

7: Eating Locally
April 13, 2010

I'm often dismayed by how little I know about crops. It's not enough just being born in the Central Valley or living here. Unless you get your hands dirty, you don't really understand farming. Even with a little vegetable garden in my backyard, I'm no farmer.

But I have learned a few things:

- Eighty percent of all agricultural sales in the United States come from four Central Valley counties: Fresno, Tulare, Kern and Merced.
- One in every four mouthfuls of food consumed in this country comes from here.
- We rank number one among all the states in production of fruits and vegetables.

With all those customers, why is it so important for us to buy locally grown food here? Well, first of all, it tastes better. Anyone who's ever eaten a fresh fruit or a vegetable knows that.

Second, it's better for you. I don't just mean better for your health. I'm talking about the bigger better. Because by supporting our own community, we recycle limited resources. Think of it as a sort of organic karma. You've heard the expression, "What goes around comes around." Well, how about this: "What GROWS around STAYS around."

Of course, we don't need to be fanatical about it. There's nothing immoral about eating the occasional apple from Sonoma or New York or even New Zealand. But I want my grapes to ripen on nearby vines. I prefer my raisins to dry under the Central California sunshine. And I like a nice French Beaujolais. But the Fresno State Winery produces some excellent vino.

So, here's my bit of unsolicited advice: The next time you go in search of sustenance, remember its roots. Support your local farmer.

8: Buying Locally
April 20, 2010

Today, we've been talking about obesity and diabetes. As we heard, those two health problems are closely related. Of course, not every diabetic is obese and not every obese person gets diabetes. There is a clear link between obesity and myriad diseases. Diabetes is only one.

Most people who listen to public radio tend to be better educated and more concerned about their health. So, you probably already knew much of what we were discussing this past hour. Whether you learned something today or not, I hope you'll pass on this information to others.

Now, here's something you might not know. Buying food is one of the most important decisions you make. Naturally, it affects your health and the well-being of your family. But there's more.

Every time you buy something to eat, it impacts the entire food chain. The retailer records a sale and is more like to re-order that item. The distributor does the same thing. So does the producer. Whether you switch from one brand of corn flakes to another or, say, suddenly start eating organic fruits and vegetables, it motivates the grocer, the sales clerk, the stocker, the truck driver, the warehouse operator, the farmer, the fertilizer companies, the farm workers, the farm machinery manufacturers, their families, and everyone with they all do business.

The way you buy food also matters. Have you noticed the increase in self check-out lanes at supermarkets? Well, each one of those robotic checkers is one human job being eliminated. We know that unemployment is at record levels. Some critics say the government should create more jobs. Well, here's something you can do: Refuse to use the self check-out lane. It might be inconvenient to wait a bit longer, but you'll send a message to store owners that you support more jobs for people, not machines. Besides, why should we have to check out our own groceries? If we're going to scan bar codes, I think the store should pay us to operate that equipment. I mean, really.

One last thing: I want to go on record as being opposed to infomercials selling weight loss without diet and exercise. If you're like me and want to lose a few pounds or a lot of pounds, don't waste ten cents of your money or ten minutes or your time on those false promises of burning fat with pills, gadgets or any other nonsense. There is only one formula for losing weight: eat less and exercise more. It's hard work, but if I can do it, so can you.

9: Bottom Line
September 29, 2006

So, what have we learned about agriculture? Well first of all, milk is not the only thing
that comes out of cows. They also produces some things you don't want to step in;
others you don't want to breathe in. But we do need cows.

Second, not all crops come wrapped in plastic. Some of them actually come up out of
the ground.

And third, crops are not the only things that come up out of the ground. We pump oil
and water. And then there are the houses, springing up like wildflowers, because more
and more of us want to live here.

You know, it takes more than good soil, good weather and good luck to grow good
crops. It also takes hard work and lots of careful planning. Unless we're careful, our
Central Valley could turn into a place where abundant farming is a memory. That
means keeping a careful balance between food and shelter.

It's important to farmers, of course. But in the end, it's important to us all. Because
there's only so much land and air and water to go around.

SICKNESS AND HEALTH

10: Air Quality
March 4, 2008

There are few things more fundamental to our quality of life than the air we breathe. I have often thought that if beings from some advanced civilization were to visit our planet, they would conclude we were (to put it mildly) insane.

What intelligent species would intentionally poison its own atmosphere? Apart from the fact that air pollution kills us, it exacerbates every other problem we have, from illness to blight. You'd think this was so obvious we would never even consider dumping garbage into the air and water and soil.

Well, think again. Since Adam and Eve first tossed that proverbial apple core onto the ground, we've been sullying our planet. Don't worry, we seem to say. Someone else will clean it up.

I'm sorry, but there is not one else. We are the clean-up crew. And if we don't hurry, there might not be much left to clean. Every day, we are destroying what is left of our neighborhoods, our cities, our state, our world. You might not care about that. But I do. So please, stop it. Listen to you mother. Clean up after yourself.

11: Recycling
February 17, 2009

San Joaquin Valley has the worst air quality in California, maybe in America. Our dirty atmosphere is responsible for an acceleration of illness, with more sick days at work and school, more trips to the doctor, earlier and longer hospital stays, as well as shorter life expectancy. People suffer and die from asthma, emphysema, pneumonia, bronchitis, diabetes and stroke -- all caused or exacerbated by air pollution. And let's be clear about this: It's not simply a quirk of weather or topography. We put poisons in our atmosphere.

I remember the first Earth Day: April 22, 1970. We began to focus national attention on our growing environmental problems. Nearly forty years ago, I'm not sure how much progress we've made. The missing element is still a sense of personal responsibility.

On Sunday, the Bakersfield Californian published a front-page story under the headline, "Why Can't We Recycle Like Fresno?" The newspaper noted that every home in Fresno has a recycling bin. In Bakersfield, residents who want curbside recycling must pay four dollars a month. That's about thirteen cents a day. Yet only seven percent of households participate.

When asked whether more should be done to encourage recycling, twelve percent of Bakersfield respondents said no. But more than half of those surveyed (59 percent) said the service should be free.

OK, I get it. A lot of people don't want to pay for public services. A lot of people don't want to pay for anything. Well, good luck getting anyone to clean up the mess for free. And good luck with all the other costs you incur. Because without recycling, we must use more natural resources and energy and land. So, the next time you wonder why the cost of everything is going up, just remember that you didn't want to spend thirteen cents a day for a big blue box. Yeah, that was a good idea.

I leave you with this thought: If we're not careful, those words by Emma Lazarus on the Statue of Liberty might soon apply to us -- the huddled masses yearning to breathe free.

Today, we've been talking about the state of our drug policy. There's more to this topic than the controlled substances banned by law. Consider caffeine, nicotine and alcohol. Each one kills more people than all the so-called hard drugs combined.

So, how do we discourage the abuse of such substances? Well, we know what happens when we try to prohibit them. Organized crime happens. And yet, we do prohibit them. And of course, there is a lot of crime. And of course, people continue to consume them.

Which brings me to one of my favorite subjects: knowledge versus ignorance. I've always found it odd that the first lesson taught in the Bible is that knowledge is a bad thing. You remember Eve and Adam. They were booted out of paradise because they chose to eat that prohibited apple from the tree of knowledge. And why did they do it? Simple: They wanted information that they were not allowed to have.

Here's a thought: Maybe the snake was right. Eating that apple gave inhabitants of Eden the one thing that makes me proud to be human: our ability to think. We might not use that ability very well or very often. But at least it gives us a chance to do better than we might by remaining ignorant.

Throughout history, authority figures have tried to hide information from people. Religious leaders always tell us why heathens are bad, but often fail to tell us why they might also be good. Politicians always give us reasons to oppose political adversaries, but usually leave out any reasons to support them. Military commanders motivate troops to hate the enemy, but not to love their fellow man.

And so it goes with drugs. In the 1920s, we had demon rum. In the 30s, it was reefer madness. Never mind that both alcohol and pot have medicinal value.

During the 1940s and 50s, tobacco was touted as a curative. Today, cigarettes are evil. But does anyone remember that nicotine also has beneficial properties?

I leave you with this question: Why is the pharmaceutical industry one of the biggest businesses on earth? Maybe drugs aren't the problem. Maybe ignorance is.

13: Our Common Problem
November 6, 2005

Unlike the weather, we can do something concerning our health besides just talk about it. And it doesn't take much to make a big difference in our well being. Relatively small changes in diet, exercise and so-called lifestyle habits can lead to rather dramatic improvements in the way we feel.

On the other hand, it doesn't take much to feel worse, either. Sometimes our health deteriorates simply by doing nothing. Thomas Jefferson wrote that all men are created equal. In reality, we have neither equal genetics, nor equal resources, nor equal access to health care. Those things also make a huge difference in how well -- and how long -- we live.

On a personal note, I'm ashamed to admit that although we live in the richest country on earth, a huge percentage of our fellow citizens still get sick and die largely because they can't afford proper health care. According to the Census Bureau, more than 45 million Americans -- that's one in six of us -- have absolutely no medical insurance. The percentage is even higher among those of us who earn less than $25,000 a year. One in four are uninsured.

The World Health Organization says we have the most expensive health care system on the planet. The United States is the only developed nation except South Africa not to provide health care for every citizen. Overall, we rank very low.

By contrast, we are in first place by far when it comes to military spending. Last year, the United States comprised almost half of the entire world's combined armed services budgets. Half. Yet, we're cutting medical benefits for military personnel and veterans. It's a shameful way to treat those men and women who have dedicated their lives to protect us.

Now, this country clearly does not lack the financial resources to provide better health care for all of our people. We simply don't give it the highest priority. In my opinion, the time is long past due to resolve that inequity.

14: Personal Responsibility
February 16, 2010

When the subject of medical care comes up, I often hear the opinion that people should take individual responsibility for their health. I agree with that idea. For example, there's not much point in treating somebody for obesity if he or she refuses to try losing weight through diet and exercise. Or giving a lung transplant to someone who smokes cigarettes.

But what about the health of our society? Don't we have some obligation as citizens to improve our environment by putting fewer pollutants into the atmosphere? Some folks doubt the scientific evidence regarding the dangers of excess industrial emissions. Well, maybe they're not worried about climate change. But how about emphysema, cystic fibrosis, asthma, heart disease or stroke? Those are all caused or exacerbated by air pollution.

This is not speculation. These are facts. We've reached the point in our evolution as a species when ignorance is no longer an excuse. It's time to take responsibility for our behavior. If you saw someone throwing garbage into your home, you'd tell them to stop. Every day, we see garbage being put into our air. It's time to say stop.

I don't know about you, but I'd like to live long enough to see the day when the Central Valley does not lead the list of most polluted regions in the United States. Let's start now. This is not a political. Democrats or Republicans, left or right, it doesn't matter.

If you consider yourself liberal, try liberating yourself from that automobile once in a while. Put fewer hydrocarbons into your life's exhaust system without waiting for the government to pass more laws or raise taxes.

If you consider yourself conservative, try conserving energy. You'll save your lungs. You'll improve the chances of leaving behind a habitable planet for your descendants. And by the way, you'll also save money. And after all, isn't that the American way?

<u>15: European Model</u>
June 23, 2009

Today, we've been focusing on the availability of medical services in the Central Valley. Health care is something we talk about every month on "Quality of Life."

I recently spent some time in Europe and was reminded about one of the main differences between us. In Britain, France, Germany and the other 27 member states of the E-U, health care is a guaranteed right of all citizens. Here, medical care is really a privilege. We live in the only rich country on earth without universal health care.

Many Americans worry that implementing any government health care plan would lead to lower quality based on a fear of socialism. Well, let me give you some facts.

Some of the best and most economic medical care in the world is provided by a big government agency called the Veterans Administration, widely considered to be the highest-quality healthcare provider in the United States.

In this country, if you lose your job, retire or relocate, you can lose your health insurance benefits. Unless you are independently wealthy, it's possible to die because you're too poor to see a private doctor but not poor enough to see a public doctor.

Compared to people in other rich countries, most Americans are in poor health particularly in the areas of infant mortality and overall life expectancy. Europeans, Japanese and Canadians all stand a better chance of surviving birth, and all live longer than we do.

The World Health Organization continues to give the United States low scores in medical services and overall health, falling below most other industrialized nations. We pay a lot but we get relatively little.

Medicine in America is a big business. That's why so many Americans remain uninsured or underinsured. It's just not profitable to take care of them. The bottom line is that in this country, your provider decides what care you get based on their financial interests, not yours.

So, can we improve our medical care? Maybe. It depends on us. There has never been a more important time to contact our representatives in Washington and to demand that they put our interests ahead of theirs. We should remind them that if they don't, the next election is only sixteen months away.

16: The Good Old Days
February 27, 2007

Many people long for the good old days. That's especially true regarding medicine.
Well, I hate to be the one to break this to you, but there were no good old days. A one-horse town doctor fifty years ago did not cure illness better than today's HMO staff physicians with state-of-the-art equipment. Marcus Welby was an invention of ABC-TV.

On the other hand, we do face a health care catastrophe. It's the same one looming ahead for energy, transportation and the environment. And it all has to do with money.
There are too many people chasing too few resources. Unless somebody comes up with a solution soon, a lot more of us are going to be very, very sick -- and very, very unhappy. Granted, a large number of patients in our medical care system are being treated for illness caused by their own lifestyle choices. Whether it's cigarette smoking, overeating, alcohol abuse or lack of exercise, we need to take responsibility for our health.

Having said that, I believe we have a moral obligation to provide basic health care for everyone. Please notice I said "basic" health care. That means anyone who has need for first aid or who has an infectious disease should be entitled to proper attention. That includes such things as a regular check-up, medical advice and primary preventive care -- paid for by all of us. That's because it is to our mutual benefit to keep everybody healthy. The problem becomes what to do for those with more difficult health problems.
Treating a broken bone is one thing. Curing cancer is quite another.

Now, I'm not sure where you draw the line between essential care and extravagant care. Unfortunately, we do not have unlimited funds. Private companies can't shoulder the entire burden, and there's a limit to how much we're willing to pay in taxes. So, until someone comes up with an affordable way to provide universal coverage for everything from the common cold to chemotherapy, I say we should focus our attention on the immediate, fundamental needs.

The hard fact is that we all will die someday. But there is no justification for people in this country to die simply because they were too poor to get basic medical attention.
That's not just immoral; it's stupid.

17: Cure vs. Prevention
June 15, 2010

I often wonder why we don't spend more resources on prevention instead of waiting until problems get bad before curing them. I suppose it's human nature. We tend to put our energies into short-term interests. You know, things like weight-loss pills or surgery rather than diet and exercise.

Here's one of my pet peeves. I can't tell you how many times I've watched people leave empty shopping carts in a parking lot rather than returning them to the store. It would be such an easy way to prevent problems like dents and scratched paint, not to mention taking up limited parking space. I guess some folks just can't be bothered walking a few extra steps. And yet, those very same people suffer the consequences from the discourtesy of others. Go figure.

Now, that's not a crucial problem, I suppose. But when it comes to our health, we often ignore the long-term benefits of developing good personal habits early in life. That also applies to the medical care decisions we make as a society.

I was disappointed to watch last year's debate end without any form of universal health insurance. Once again, we opted for short-term greed instead of long-term benefits. I don't know if our country will ever reach the level of maturity exhibited by many other developed nations. I hope so. Meanwhile, I guess it's up to us as individuals to do the right thing.

So, until and unless we provide affordable basic medical care for everyone, we'll just have to manage the best we can for ourselves.

<u>18: Nursing Homes</u>
July 21, 2009

Today, we've been talking about skilled rehabilitation facilities known by various names: nursing homes, convalescent homes, rest homes. Over the years, I've visited friends and relatives in such places, and must admit to having a certain bias.

Despite all the good that they do, these facilities always make me feel sad, in part because their residents are not well. Patients are too sick to go to their own homes. Sometimes, people die in these places. Then there are the sounds and the smells. Moans of anxiety and agony. Odors of human waste and disinfectant chemicals.

Finally, there's the attitude. Workers must deal with a variety of problems: demands for more medication, complaints about the food, climate controls, even poor television reception, all exacerbated by inadequate staffing and supervision.

One of my best friends passed away a couple months ago. Bob Brown and I had worked together at the Pacific Telephone Company back in 1979. I always called him "boss" and he always called me "kid" -- right up until the very end.

Bob was born in Chicago and grew up in Bakersfield. He'd been a newspaper reporter and a PR man. The last time I saw Bob was at a nursing home in San Jose. After hip replacement surgery, his recuperation went badly. I suspect it was due in part to the poor conditions in that low-cost rehab center. The place was unpleasant to say the least.

I don't mean to criticize every nursing home. Some are truly wonderful. They all have a difficult job to do and many of their employees are outstanding. But let's face it: what you pay does affect what you get. With so many patients shuttling in and out of less expensive facilities, who could possibly expect to get excellent care? Of course, those who have the means can get private rooms with round-the-clock attention. For everyone else, unfortunately, that is not the case.

The challenge of improving America's medical care system has beleaguered our best and brightest minds. Some say leave well enough alone. Others say tear it down and start from scratch. I think the answer lies somewhere in the middle. We do have excellent care providers, excellent facilities, excellent medication. What we lack is access. The goal should be to give everyone guaranteed excellent basic health care. That should include excellent rehabilitation services. Beyond that, everyone may be entitled to get the medical services they can afford, whether through insurance or personal resources.

The mistake is letting the marketplace determine the quality of care. There's should be no room for poor treatment at any price, even a cut-rate one.

March 16, 2010

Today, we've been talking about a couple of very serious subjects, teen pregnancy and domestic violence. Although most of us are not directly affected by either of these social issues, they both have an impact on our quality of life.

Regardless of one's views on religion, most parents consider the birth of a child to be a blessing. Babies bring great joy into life. If that were not the case, who would intentionally go through the myriad difficulties of having children?

There was a time in human history when people did not understand how the human reproductive system worked. Thousands of years ago, pregnancy was explained as simply an act of God. Today, we know a bit more and people can choose how, when, or even whether to have children. Science doesn't make the birth of babies less blessed, just less mysterious.

That's why I'm puzzled by some folks disregarding what they know in favor of what was formerly taken on faith. The only thing worse than deliberate personal unawareness is the institutional enforcement of ignorance. In a free country, family planning should not require permission from church or state. To make it a political issue is just silly.

What does make sense it to think about the consequences of having kids. Mothers and fathers affect not their own lives and that of their children, but everyone else's, too. The quality of our public education, health care, safety -- in fact, almost all aspects of our society -- can be attributed to parenting skills. And as we've learned, unwanted pregnancy can even lead to domestic violence.

I was very fortunate to have terrific parents. Who I am is largely due to how their raised me. Maybe I haven't measured up to their exact expectations, and maybe I don't speak from great experience as the father of many children, but I am proud to be the son of great parents. So, if you don't like my opinion, take it up with them.

20: Going Boldly
August 18, 2009

In the national debate over health care reform, there is a sharp divide between the generous majority and a selfish minority. On the generous side, most people are in favor of a single-payer, universal insurance system where the government guarantees payment but where the providers are mostly in private practice. Medical decisions stay between doctors and patients.

Those on the greedy side want to continue the status quo. Frankly, I don't understand why anyone would want that unless they worked for an insurance company. Doctors want reform. Hospitals want reform. And most importantly, the majority of patients want reform.

Despite what some say, there is no conflict here between personal liberty and social responsibility. Democrats and Republicans generally agree that all Americans should have affordable access to competent health care. In proposed legislation, the main role of government would simply be to guarantee payment for that care. Private insurance companies could continue to provide stop-gap coverage, just as with Medicare. Just as in Canada, Japan and dozens of European countries. It's not (you should pardon the expression) brain surgery.

I'm confused by all this apparent controversy. For example, I've heard many people say they do not want the government to start rationing medicine. Obviously, those people are unaware that we already have rationed health care. Only the rich and powerful get unlimited, round-the-clock treatment. The rest of us are subject to some rational limitations. And by the way, when did the word "rational" become a bad thing?

Come on. This is the United States of America. We landed on the moon. We won the Cold War. We even figured out how to make an instant coffee that I like. So why, in the 21st century, can we not find a way to agree on universal health care? Can't we just tell our representatives to pass a damned health bill?

OK. We're not living in the utopia of Star Trek. Yet, this country stands shamefully alone in failing to ensure care for the least among us. I know we can solve this problem. After all, the rest of the civilized world already has universal health care. It's not as if we're trying to boldly go where no one has gone before.

21: Golden Rule
October 23, 2007

For the past two weeks, we've been talking about the most important domestic issue in America today: the cost of health care. But how much care do we want? How much do we need?

My personal opinion is that we should treat medical care the same way we treat other core elements affecting the quality of life. Take just two examples: education and public safety. Both are considered essential to our well-being. Both cost money. Both are given very high priority in our political system.

In the case of schools, we provide an elementary and even secondary level of instruction for all our children. We require kids to attend classes and pass tests. Of course, anyone also has the right to send his or her child to a private school.

Public safety is much the same. Police and firefighters defend us against natural and manmade risks. They require us to comply with the law and behave with prudence. Fire departments even provide some emergency medical care with paramedics. On the other hand, individuals and businesses also have the right to hire private guards, implement security systems, or install fire suppression equipment.

We consider a fundamental level of protection and education to be in the community's best interest. Public medical care should be no different. Our very existence depends on fighting disease, treating injuries, preventing health risks. I understand there is no simple answer to how we pay for such services. But it's time to stop thinking of doctors and nurses and clinics and hospitals as luxuries. Along with teachers and police officers and firefighters, medical care professionals help to ensure that one word which comes before liberty and the pursuit of happiness: life.

Today, we've been talking about running for fun and for health. I ran cross-country when I was in high school. In those days, we didn't use any special equipment or advanced training, just a pair of sneakers and as much lung power as we could muster. Now, I'm not what you'd call a great athlete. I never was. My best mile took about seven or eight minutes. I accepted the fact that I would not necessarily be the fastest or the strongest kid on the field.

And in a way, that's been my philosophy ever since. I like to win, but I'm much less obsessed with winning, less aggressive than I used to be.

The desire to be best is typically Americans. We are a super competitive country. You might say our national personality is type-A. We've all known such individuals: the relentless boss, the perfectionist co-worker. I wonder how much that spirit contributes to a person's early demise. Can the need to lead cause more stress than satisfaction? Produce heart attacks and strokes? I don't know.

I do know a little bit about marathons. The word comes from the Battle of Marathon, *Marathón* being the name of an old Greek city-state where the Greco-Persian wars were fought about twenty-five hundred years ago. According to legend, a messenger was sent to announce the Greek victory there. His name was Phillipidis which, by the way, was also my family's original surname.

As the story goes, this ancestor of mine ran all the way without stopping, told the Greeks our soldiers had won, *Neníkikamen!* Then he collapsed and died. So much for winning.

One of my favorite Greek sayings is, "Pan metrion aristo." It means, "Moderation in all things." Can one be both excellent and moderate? I think so. On the other hand, I believe extremism is a terrible vice. With all due respect to Barry Goldwater, that's even true regarding the defense of liberty.

So, here's my unsolicited advice to you: Run if you like. Compete if you wish. Be first if you can. But don't let it kill you.

23: Longevity
November 2, 2010

I suppose it's true that I gravitate toward the past. Call me nostalgic, but I do miss the good old days. Even those days before my own time. I love the music, the comedy, the movies and, of course, those wonderful programs from the golden age of radio.

There are many great quotations about age. George Bernard Shaw said, "Youth is wasted on the young."

Benjamin Franklin wrote, "Life's tragedy is that we get old too soon and wise too late."

This one is attributed to Jack Benny among others: "Age is strictly a case of mind over matter. If you don't mind, it doesn't matter." That from a guy who was forever 39.

When James Thurber was about my age, he said he'd "developed inflammation of the sentence structure and a definite hardening of the paragraphs." I can appreciate that.

So what about my question: What does old mean? On his 85th birthday, the American financier Bernard Baruch was quoted in the London Observer as saying, "To me, old age is always fifteen years older than I am." That sounds about right.

If I've learned nothing else over the years, it is this: There is no escaping time. We're all stuck right now. So, we might as well enjoy this moment while it lasts.

Two last quotations about age. First, George Burns (or one of his writers) who said, "If you live to be one hundred, you've got it made. Very few people die past that age."

And finally, this one: "It's amazing, when you look at the obituaries. So many people are dying who never died before." That was said by my godfather, Albert Kabrielian. Thanks, Uncle Al.

September 14, 2010

One of the peculiar things about our society is the way we talk about death. Most of us treat it as separate from life, a sort of alien condition. Of course, there's nothing more natural or more universal than dying. With its clichéd counterpart -- taxes -- we know that death cannot be avoided. Only Fresno writer William Saroyan famously said as he lay dying that he believed God would exempt him. And in fact, that is the way most of us treat death. Everyone else must die. Not me. Not me.

This past weekend marked the ninth anniversary of the infamous September Eleventh attacks. My friend Richard Isaacs, who died this year, used to remind me that as he looked out of his Manhattan apartment and watched the twin towers going down in a jet fuel inferno, he quipped with typical New York nonchalance, "We didn't like those buildings anyway."

But, of course, for most Americans, the horror of that day was all the tragic deaths. Young people. Innocent people. Thousands of people most of whom had nothing to do with any alleged injustices which led to that attack. They were simply, unfortunately there. In the wrong place at the wrong time.

Statistically, the 9-11 victims were a small fraction of all the Americans who died in 2001. It wasn't just the number. We were shocked by the injustice of those civilian casualties. We were also awakened from a slumber of self-confidence in our national security. But rather than marshalling the immeasurable international good-will, we snubbed our friends, provoked our adversaries, and worst of all, unjustly punished our fellow citizens and killed thousands more innocents abroad.

Each one of those wounded and dead deserved better from us. We did not need to make a bad situation so much worse. And yet, here we are. Still hip-deep in death and destruction. Still squandering out limited resources. Still no light at the end of this long, dark tunnel.

I'm optimistic by nature, skeptical by training, and inquisitive by preference. I do believe we can overcome our strained relationships at home and overseas. I'm not sure how our country will manage that. But I am here to tell you that we can do it as individuals.

On Saturday, I had the pleasure of visiting the Bakersfield mosque on Ming Avenue. I was welcomed at that Islamic house of worship. A lot of other non-Muslims were there, too, including some Christian clergy and their families. There were no harsh words, no antagonism, only warmth and hospitality. That is how people overcome their suspicions and fears by getting to know each other.

By forming individual bonds, we can overcome the mob mentality. That's the way to stop fascists from burning books and exhorting us to war. We can't stop death. But we can improve our quality of life.

<u>25: Death and Dying</u>
March 11, 2008

Throughout the ages, we have been using the seasons of the year as a metaphor to describe the times of our lives. Spring is birth. Summer is youth. Autumn is maturity. Winter is death.

So it should come as no surprise that Easter and Passover coincide approximately with the vernal equinox -- a time for resurrection, if you will.

I recently heard a priest talking about the coming holidays. He said that people often ask him, "When will the world end?"

Strictly speaking, when someone dies, the world ends for that person. Metaphorically speaking, each of us dies a little bit when a loved one is lost. More and more people are choosing to determine the time and manner of their own death. The law has been slow to accept that tendency. Maybe it's our fear of the unknown. But if we live long enough, we inevitably have to deal with it.

So far, I have not met anyone who could convincingly tell me what happens after we die. Even those who have technically died on an operating table -- then have been revived -- can only assume that their own recollections are accurate. Apart from religious beliefs, we are left to wonder. It's not very satisfying to have such a universally unanswerable question. Which is why, I suppose, most of us accept the traditions of our ancestors on faith.

So, here's a modest proposal: Let's stop fighting over the things we can't possibly know. Let's just live and let live while we're alive -- and when we pass on, let's live and let die.

February 23, 2010

Today, we've been talking about death. It's one of those subjects which we rarely discuss or even think about. Maybe that's why dying comes as such a shock. It's certainly should be no surprise. On the contrary, we ought to be astonished if we never die. But you and I tacitly agree with William Saroyan, assuming that God will make an exception in our case.

In truth, eventually, each of us will stop breathing. Our hearts will stop beating. Our brains will stop functioning. We will die.

Nevertheless, most of us behave as if we were immortal. That's true as individuals and it's true collectively. We think of ourselves and of our groups as having no end. My family, my country, my species will last forever. Do we have any evidence to think that is so? On the contrary, all the previous examples should logically lead us to conclude that we will go the way of every other creature. The one thing we can assuredly count on is ultimate extinction.

Now, I realize that this notion interferes with many religious teachings. It's rather comforting to believe we will see our departed loves again, that we, ourselves, have an eternal life waiting for us beyond the grave.

We don't like the idea that some things are unknown and unknowable. We reject the thesis that things cease to be. We reinforce such feelings by building monuments to ourselves, by engaging in ceremonies of perpetuity and celebrations of time without end. We reassure each other that good-bye should be *hasta la vista* and not *adios*.

I don't know what follows this reality. Maybe it's something. Maybe it's nothing. Maybe it's void. Maybe it's not.

But if immortality is important to you, here are three ways to approach it:

1. Donate blood while you're still alive.
2. Donate your organs and tissues when you die.
3. Teach someone to read.

These simple things might not give you everlasting life on earth. But you'll quickly provide a better quality of life for others. And you'll improve the world for a long time to come.

RICHER OR POORER

<u>27: Gregory Phillipidis</u>
February 24, 2009

If he were still alive, my father would have been 88 years old today. Gregory Phillipidis was born in Smyrna, Greece. That city is now called Izmir, Turkey. Dad's name was changed to Phillips when he became a U.S. citizen.

My father spoke many languages including Greek, Turkish, Arabic, Italian, Spanish and English. He grew up in Alexandria, Egypt. After World War Two, Dad traveled around the world as a merchant seaman. He loved to haggle. One of his pastimes was visiting flea markets.

It is often said that some people seem to have a special knack for doing business. Greeks, Armenians, Arabs and Jews have this reputation. But, of course, the whole world is a marketplace.

We are witnessing a moment in history when free trade on our planet seems not to be functioning normally. Is this the result of too much regulation or not enough regulation? I don't know. I do know that what we need is Goldilocks regulation. It should be just right.

I leave you with this thought: International economic forces are inextricably interrelated. Sooner or later, we must accept the fact that what happens to our economy happens to everyone. There is no us and them. It's only us.

28: Capitalism
April 14, 2009

How much money is enough? The patriarch of American capitalism, John D. Rockefeller, reportedly was once asked that question. How much money is enough? He answered, "More."

A market used to be the place where one exchanged money for goods. Today, the market often refers to a place where one trades money for the prospect of making more money. Goods are not only purchased for their intrinsic value. They are bought and sold in hopes of profiting from their increased -- or in some cases, their decreased value.

In my lifetime, the practice of investment has become almost ubiquitous and now applies to almost anything. We've gone from a mostly cash-based economy 50 years ago to one based largely on credit, which is to say, on debt.

During the 1990s, I remember watching currency in the former Soviet Union go from ten rubles per dollar to more than six thousand. Talk about an economic crisis! To compensate, many Russians bought imported consumer electronics such as VCRs and TV sets to lock in the value of their money. They later sold or bartered those commodities without losing much to inflation.

As a young man, I was told to save money. In principle, a prudent person was supposed to have enough squirreled away to live for a year without working. Today, many live from paycheck to paycheck without saving anything. They hold fantastic hopes of making a big score someday. Well, here's a news flash for you: Most people do not get rich quickly -- neither on the stock market nor in a casino.

I leave you with these facts: The odds of winning the California Super Lotto Jackpot are 1 in 18 million. So, if you buy 50 Lotto tickets each week, statistically you'll win the jackpot about once every 5,000 years. Good luck with that!

<u>29: Greed</u>
December 8, 2009

Today, we've been talking about some of the ways that commercial companies help their local communities. You might say this topic was a sequel to our last program which focused on personal service.

I've often wondered why some people chose to give of themselves while others tend to be rather greedy. In the movie "Wall Street" starring Michael Douglas as successful broker Gordon Gekko. His character tells us, "Greed is good." Time and again, we hear that the guiding principle of our free enterprise system is to maximize profit. The customer might always be right, but that slogan is meaningless if it doesn't improve the bottom line.

So, what happened to the virtue of sacrifice? Religions teach us to practice altruism in this life in exchange for reward in the next. The faithful are supposed to reject avarice. Yet, materialism frequently clashes with so-called sacred values. The sanctimonious trumps the divine.

My favorite example of this is health care. The on-going debate keeps coming back to a question of economics. I understand that we don't have unlimited financial resources. But should money always be more important than medicine? I think our society's first priority ought to be helping those who are least able to help themselves. Instead, I see the wealthiest few guaranteeing that they keep what they have -- and those who wish to be rich going along in hopes that they, too, will be rich someday. Isn't that how this mess got started?

Ebenezer Scrooge would be proud.

30: Generosity
December 21, 2010

Today we've been talking about micro-credit and philanthropy. It's often said that the measure of a great society is how it treats those who have the least, those who need the most. It's easy to be generous in good times. It's also relatively painless for a rich person to give the same amount as one of modest means.

Then again, what does "rich" mean? I recently asked that question of a friend who is, by most standards, very well off. He owns lots of property, lives in a large, comfortable house, has millions of dollars in the bank and can do essentially whatever he wants. This friend who shall remain nameless admits that he is rich. But he told me he does not consider himself to be that rich. Compared to others in the world, he says his wealth is limited.

My friend is quite benevolent. And yet, even he does not give as much proportionately as many others who have much less money. Does that make him a scrooge? Does that make the less wealthy person a spendthrift?

And by the way, why do we give away that which is ours? Well, in addition to tax incentives and peer pressure, I think generosity is motivated by what is in one's heart. Munificence makes us feel good. But we do have another reason to help others. Generosity is actually a selfish act. By coming to the aid of our fellows in need, we improve the entire society.

In the end, we are better off when everyone prospers. In the end, goodwill is actually quite logical. Unlike greed, which is simply short-sighted, mean and stupid. So, the next time you hear someone say he's for tax cuts, perhaps you should question his common sense.

Anyway, that is my two cents' worth.

<u>31: Labor</u>
September 4, 2007

I think all of us at one time or another have wanted to tell a boss or a supervisor or some other authority figure those two magic words: "I quit."

And why not? That is the very principle upon which this country was founded. The Declaration of Independence was our way of telling King George the Third, "We quit." Over the years, we have walked away from many things: the League of Nations, treaties with American Indians, the Kyoto Agreement.

The right to quit is very important to us. We routinely encourage people around the world to leave the chains of bondage and overthrow dictators. In 1991, America cheered as all fifteen Soviet republics separated from the USSR.

On the other hand, we don't always honor that right. Take our own Civil War. Some argue the Confederate States should have been able to secede legally from the Union. President Lincoln disagreed. Honest Abe freed the slaves, but the South remained part of the United States. No quitting allowed there.

As individuals, we do have the right to quit. You can leave home, leave a marriage, resign from public office. You can even leave the country. But as a practical matter, it's very difficult to quit a job. The system is designed to discourage quitting. You lose your income, of course. Depending on the circumstances, you might also lose your medical insurance, your pension, and a variety of other benefits.

That's where unions come in. At one time, they helped introduce child labor laws, overtime, the minimum wage, and a number of other protections for workers.

The role of organized labor has changed over the years. Recently, we've seen many unions dwindle in membership and effectiveness. Nevertheless, the power of collective bargaining is still a powerful element in the relations between labor and management.

In the end, your right to join might be even more important than your right to quit.

September 2, 2008

My father was a lifelong member of the plumbers and steamfitters union, local 39 in San Jose. He taught me that organized labor protected the rights of workers, helped improve job conditions, wages and benefits. I, myself, am a member of AFTRA, a union that represents radio and television performers.

So, with all this history, you might naturally expect me to have a strong bias in favor of organized labor. And you might be wrong.

On one hand, I do support the right of workers to organize. I'm strongly in favor of a living minimum wage, health care, a good retirement plan and many of the other benefits associated with unions.

On the other hand, I am very disappointed by the deterioration of unions over the past few decades. There was a time when the majority of American workers were represented by trade organizations that protected employee interests. That picture has changed. Today, a small minority of Americans belong to a union and the value of that representation is often questionable.

The biggest problem I see is this: Many unions have become so big that members need help dealing with the bureaucracy. In my case, AFTRA is of no help in this part of California since the cost to organize would outweigh any potential advantages.

Labor relations are like a three-legged stool. One leg is management, a second is labor, and a third is government regulation. Each is necessary to prevent the others from gaining too much power. Unfortunately, government and management have practically become one big leg and labor has almost nowhere to sit.

I do believe the pendulum will swing back the other way. We need a more balanced relationship between owners and employees. Fortunately, most workers in America are not abused by their bosses. But enough are that they really need help standing up for their rights. Unions are the best way to get that help. The alternative is revolution, and no sane person wants that.

33: Job Satisfaction
September 29, 2009

I've been lucky most of my life to enjoy interesting employment. The fact is that I love my work. Now, don't tell my boss, but if I didn't need the money, I'd probably do this free of charge.

Unfortunately, as with most people, I do need money. About ten years ago, I came into a bit of a windfall. For a short while, I even tried to retire. And you know what? I hated it. Turns out I thrive on working. And when you think about it, that's not surprising.

I grew up in a culture that valued work. Slothfulness was not only discouraged. It was considered a sin. On the other hand, there is such a thing as too much diligence. Many of us who can't leave the office become workaholics.

In addition to earning a living, I think most of us work to feel satisfied. A job gives a person a certain status. The most common question you ask when you meet someone in this country is, "What do you do?" Which is shorthand for, "Who are you?"

I was fortunate to discover who I was early in life. Journalism came naturally to me. I've always enjoyed writing and asking questions and telling stories. I hope to keep doing this as long as I draw breath.

For many years, I ended each broadcast report with the same words -- to the point where they became synonymous with my name. In those days, I wasn't just Terry Phillips. I was "Terry Phillips, CBS News, Moscow." It wasn't just my job. It was my identity.

That's still true today. My job is quite literally what I do for a living. I live to work because I am my work. If I were ever unemployed, it would be an identity crisis.

The older I get, the more I wonder what else I should be doing while I'm still alive. So far, I haven't found anything that beats what I'm doing right now. I try taking time for vacations. But in many ways, my job is a vacation. Lucky me, right?

So, what's my point? I guess what I'm trying to say is that I understand why unemployment is such a big problem. It's not only about the money. Work gives us purpose. And if we're lucky, it gives us satisfaction.

This week, the U.S. Financial Crisis Inquiry Commission is due to release its final report on the causes behind our current economic mess. That bipartisan panel was appointed in 2009 by Congress, and chaired by former California State Treasurer Phil Angelides. The Commission's Vice Chair, former Congressman Bill Thomas, used to represent parts of the Central Valley.

The Financial Crisis Inquire Commission interviewed more than seven hundred witnesses. They scheduled nearly twenty public hearings including one in Bakersfield. It was a terrific opportunity for us to learn what went wrong and to prevent recurrences. Instead, what we got were bankers and brokers and others in the world of high finance saying the economy's collapse was terrible -- but not their fault.

Rather than producing a single comprehensive document, the Democrats wrote one and the Republicans wrote two others. So much for the new spirit of unity in Washington.

Everyone seems to agree on one thing: We are greedy. Americans are against government waste, but no one wants to cut public spending on the programs they like. We blame those who take from the public coffers, but we have no problem doing so when it benefits us.

Politicians don't like to vote against the desires of their constituents. But as we've learned, money is not unlimited. We won't raising taxes and we can't live in the red forever. Former Vice-President Dick Cheney was wrong. Deficits do matter.

Whether in Washington, in Sacramento or at home -- Republicans, Democrats and independents -- we all say let's control spending. But nobody wants to be the first to sacrifice. And yet, that is what we need to do. Sooner or later, one way or another, we will have to manage with less. OK, so what are you willing to give up? I thought so.

<u>35: Losing Everything</u>
August 28, 2007

We often hear people say, "This is the worst such and such crisis in history." And usually, that simply isn't true. Conditions might be bad, but there have almost always been times when conditions were worse.

Unfortunately, we find ourselves comparing bad times with worse times. On one hand, some people are doing very well. Some people always do very well -- usually, the same people. For them, these are excellent economic times.

On the other hand, some people live in fear of losing everything. For them, these are not excellent economic times.

Now, let me share a little secret with you: Wealth and wisdom do not always go together. Those who have the most money are not necessarily any wiser than the rest of us. Many rich folks are quite smart. But knowledge is not the same as wisdom. Knowing how to make money and how to keep money does not guarantee good economic judgment. Those in the minority who are super wealthy generally have no clue what the rest of us need.

As one who is not super wealthy, let me suggest that what the rest of us need is a reasonable chance to achieve the American dream. By that, I mean the following: In this country:

- People should have access to an affordable education, housing and medical care.
- People should have a chance to earn a decent living.
- People should be free to quit a job without losing everything.
- And finally, those who are unable to work should live affordably and in dignity.

I believe that in this country, no one should live in fear because they aren't rich. Is that really asking for too much?

I have a confession to make. I am addicted to Broadway shows. It doesn't matter whether they're intense dramas, hilarious comedies, musical revivals, or crazy experimental works. I love the theater.

I'm convinced that if I ever moved back to the East Coast, I would probably go broke trying to support my habit. That's because a good ticket on Broadway can cost well over $100.

The bad news is that every time I go back there, I have to budget for those expensive seats because I need my fix. The good news is that there are discount tickets available. The better news is that I don't live anywhere near New York City anymore. Of course, the best news of all is that we have plenty of excellent live performances right here.

In addition to its entertainment value, I appreciate the stage as the last bastion of free speech. Unlike any other public forum of mass communication, live theater gives playwrights and performers unfettered access to an audience -- and immediate feedback. The audience hears what you have to say and you know what they think. There are no censors, no editors and no seven-second delays. There's no need to wait for ratings, either. The ovations or the boos are instantaneous.

A stage play can be very economical. Although high technology has invaded the theater, there is really no need for a lot of expensive equipment. One person (or a handful of actors) -- standing there, speaking -- can connect with a roomful of strangers and create an unforgettable experience. A play can change the world; open people's eyes; even threaten political leaders.

Don't believe me? For decades, the United States government banned an anti-war play called "Lysistrata." It was written by the Greek playwright Aristophanes more than 400 years before the birth of Christ. The same play was also banned in 1967 by the military junta, ironically, in Greece.

Clearly, some leaders believe that words spoken on a stage can be very powerful.

I truly hope the day will not come again in this country when we give up our right to speak and to hear the truth, whether it's in newspapers or books, on radio or TV or on a stage. Because, to quote Shakespeare once more, "Every subject's duty is the king's; but every subject's soul is his own." (*Henry V*)

37: Movies
July 10, 2007

I love going to the movies. There's something magical about sitting in a dark room full of strangers, looking at the world of fantasy on that big screen. The screen isn't so big and the stories aren't so fantastic and strangers aren't so polite. Still, I love the movies.

It might not surprise you to learn that when I was a little kid, I was (how should I put this?) a bit of a ham. I enjoyed entertaining relatives. I performed in school talent shows, did magic tricks for the neighborhood kids. Eventually, I channeled this desire for ego gratification into my work on radio and television.

Perhaps it's odd, then, that I have become rather shy over the years. Despite the fact that my career has often put me in the spotlight, fame is not on my priority list. On the contrary, I cherish my privacy. Oh, don't get me wrong: I enjoy praise as much as anyone else does -- more, probably. It's nice to be appreciated. But in my mind, mere celebrity is not the same as recognition for actual accomplishment.

In our increasingly public lives, it's difficult to succeed or fail without others noticing. Of course, many of us really want to be noticed. We want to feel that we're worthy of attention, even if it's for something silly.

Some folks become famous for doing well in business or politics. Some movie stars are known for their acting abilities. Other are famous just for being famous. Occasionally, celebrities use notoriety to influence public opinion or to champion a cause. We often give them more credibility than they deserve, while ignoring the opinions or advice of those who are truly knowledgeable but not renowned.

Forty years ago, Andy Warhol predicted that "In the future, everyone will be world-famous for 15 minutes." Today's universe of ubiquitous camera phones and instant on-line videos is making that prediction come true. True, the screen isn't so big. As Norma Desmond put it, "It's the pictures that got small." But then, maybe we got small, too. Still, I will always love going to the movies.

38: Publishing
September 18, 2007

The great writer Ray Bradbury once said that if he could return to life 50 years in the future, he'd want to visit an elementary school and see if children were still being taught to read. Bradbury said he feared that reading would become a technical skill as computers became more capable of speech.

We are already a much less literate society than we once were. That doesn't bode well for writers. And it doesn't bode well for clear thinking, either. One of my elementary school teachers taught me that sloppy writing is an indication of a sloppy mind.

There does seem to be a shortage of great writing today. Of course, some best-sellers always seem to churn out lots of books. And someone has to produce all those how-to, self-improvement, chicken-soup guides for dummies, idiots and other assorted nincompoops. But literature? Hardly.

It's understandable. On the printed page, even Ernest Hemmingway, Lev Tolstoy and Jane Austin have trouble competing with video games, movies or TV shows. But computers and other high-tech devices are no substitute for the human imagination. The theater of the mind is bigger and better than any broadcast.

So, what about modern classics? Who will write them? Who will read them? Great books begin with great ideas expressed with great language. Call me conservative if you like, but I believe physical contacts are essential to being human. Tangible artifacts connect us to each other, to our past, and to a better understanding of ourselves.

Not so very long ago, most personal correspondence was done deliberately, written with paper and ink, put in an envelope, stamped and physically transported through time and space. In our high-speed world, that process has been largely replaced by intangible and impermanent text messages -- whether email, instant mail or cell phone SMS. Try showing a shoebox full of those to your children someday.

39: Value of Art
March 18, 2008

What is art worth to you?

My fifth grade teacher at Vineland Elementary School in San Jose was Al Oliver. Mr. Oliver was a very cool guy. In addition to teaching about fractions and grammar and the American Civil War, he introduced us to the Beatles and Stan Freberg and the twist. We didn't just study Hawaii. We had a luau! We didn't just learn how to read maps. We drew a scale model of the United States on the playground blacktop.

Of course, back in those halcyon days, teachers had the luxury of teaching. Students did more than prepare for state tests five days a week. Yes, I know, that was before everything changed on 9-11. It was even before everything changed on November 22, 1963.

Well, some things have not changed. The human spirit still needs outlets for expression. The soul still refuses to be stifled. Painting and poetry and dance and sculpture and theater all require artists. We can't have a civilization without such enlightenment.

A popular American president once said this: "The arts and humanities teach us who we are and what we can be. They lie at the very core of the culture of which we are a part, and they provide the foundation from which we may reach out to other cultures so that the great heritage that is ours may be enriched by -- as well as itself enrich -- other enduring traditions."

Care to guess who said those words? No, not FDR. Not John F. Kennedy. Not even Bill Clinton. It was that other lion of liberal politics, Ronald Reagan in 1987.

The arts are not the domain of the left or the right. They require both wings in order to soar. They are as American as Norman Rockwell and Robert Mapplethorpe. They are as fundamental to being human as the air we breathe.

Last week, we talked about why the arts are important; however, we did not deal with the more fundamental question: What is art?

Just as the Supreme Court justice said about pornography, you might not be able to define art, but you know it when you see it. Or do you?

Consider Michelangelo's statue of David. Is it an art form or pornography? Does commercial art qualify? Or must it be art for art's sake? Check with collectors of Andy Warhol paintings on that one.

Is a documentary film a work of art if it turns a profit? Let's ask Michael Moore. Where is the line between an opinion piece and propaganda? I published a book recently that deals with violence among Armenians in New York City 75 years ago. Coincidentally, the Armenian government violently suppressed political protesters shortly after my book was published. It's a sad commentary on that emerging democracy.

Now, I certainly hope my book will succeed financially, but does that make me a capitalist rather than a journalist? And just how much money does it take for art to lose its status as art? Are writers at the New York Times and the Wall Street journal in professional jeopardy when their corporate owners are in the black?

The First Amendment to the U.S. Constitution protects the right of free expression, whether that be speech or press, assembly or worship. It has been broadly interpreted to include other forms of communication, from dancing to doodling.

In our country, every person is entitled to think, and to share thoughts with others. Of course, as with so many other fundamentally important things in life, there are costs involved. I understand: Almost nothing is free. Nevertheless, when faced with difficult financial decisions, I hope we will always lean toward freedom.

<u>41: Paper</u>
April 7, 2009

All right, I'll admit it: I'm a pack rat. I save everything. Old nuts and bolts, pieces of twine, newspapers, candy wrappers. Everything. Because you never know when it might come in handy.

If you looked at my desk, you'd probably be appalled. How can that guy find anything in that mess? Oh, I have a filing system. To quote one of my favorite cartoon characters, Ziggy: A place for everything, and everything all over the place.

In my defense, I do know where things are -- most of the time. The problem is that I've run out of space. Actually, I ran out of space long ago. Still, I keep on saving stuff.

I firmly believe that we throw away too many things. I don't just mean paper and plastic and metal which should be recycled -- although I do also think that.

But no, I mean memories. For example, hardly anyone writes letters anymore. How do you save sentimental e-mail messages or a touching Twitter? Can computerized correspondence even be touching? In my humble opinion (or as you'd probably text it, IMHO), we need a resurgence of rhetoric, a renaissance of writing. Real writing with a pen and paper.

During my recent overseas travels, I was grateful for access to the Internet. It was a fast and relatively inexpensive way to stay in touch with folks back home. But occasionally, I just had to make a phone call, to hear a human voice -- not just key clicks. And before I returned here, I just had to send a few postcards. Those old-fashioned little photos on stiff paper with a few scrawls of ink somehow authenticated the trip.

I know that many Valley Public Radio listeners are readers and writers. So I probably won't have to twist your arm too much with this suggestion: Once a week, invest in a bit of stationery and postage and yes, some of your limited, precious time. Write a letter. I guarantee you'll make someone's day and you'll create a small memory that will be difficult to throw away.

July 14, 2009

This is the birthday of my friend and mentor, Jerome Lawrence, one of the great American playwrights. He was born on this date in 1915 and died in 2004.

Jerry Lawrence along with his collaborator, Robert E. Lee, wrote "Inherit the Wind," "Auntie Mame," "The Night Thoreau Spent in Jail" and many others.

"Inherit the Wind" was ostensibly inspired by the infamous Scopes monkey trial which tested the validity of a Tennessee law called the Butler Act. It banned the teaching of evolution as applied to the origin of the human species. On July 21, 1925, school teacher John Scopes was found guilty of breaking that law and fined $100.

The play "Inherit the Wind" was actually about intellectual freedom, the right to think. It was first produced in 1955. At that time, many Americans lived in fear of two things: communism and Senator Joseph McCarthy.

In case you don't know, McCarthy conducted hearings allegedly aimed at exposing communists in the U-S government and elsewhere. Unfortunately, many of his targets were innocent citizens whose lives were ruined by his vicious witch hunt. His name has come to be equated with reckless and demagogic attacks on a person's character or patriotism.

Tennessee's anti-evolution statute was found unconstitutional in 1927 and the Scopes conviction overturned. But that law remained on the books for another forty years. Joseph McCarthy was eventually discredited. His colleagues censured the junior senator from Wisconsin, and he died in disgrace a few years later. But McCarthyism lives on. Today, many people are still ignorant about science, politics, economics and religion.

In "Inherit the Wind," Lawrence and Lee wrote: "An idea is a greater monument than a cathedral. And the advance of man's knowledge is more of a miracle than any sticks turned to snakes, or the parting of waters!"

Now, you might not agree with them. But I believe our most important right is the right of free expression, the right to hold and present different ideas. The stage can be a very effective forum for social commentary. I consider it to be a great way to practice journalism. Of course, it's also a wonderful form of entertainment. So, if you haven't been to the theater lately, I hope you'll go soon.

Today, we've been talking about music appreciation and the use of music in movies. I have a confession to make. Most of my exposure to classical music when I was a kid came from watching cartoons. Back then, I couldn't distinguish between Bach and Beethoven. I'm always not sure I can today. And I didn't know whether it was the Hungarian Rhapsody or Rhapsody in Blue. But like many uneducated listeners, at least I knew what I liked. And to paraphrase former U.S. Supreme Court Justice Potter Stewart, I knew it when I heard it.

My fourth grade teacher Mrs. Robertson once talked about a student who complained that he didn't like Shakespeare. She said, "You don't know what you like. You like what you know." I later learned that she borrowed that quotation from art historian Ernst Gombrich.

Why is it so important for us to know who wrote what, when and where? All good journalism students are taught that the five Ws are essential ingredients to reporting the news. But even if we're not planning to make a career in music, let alone classical music, it's useful to know about our roots. Throughout history and around the world, music has been an important part of every culture. You might say it helps define us as a species, part of what makes us uniquely human.

I also believe music appreciation enhances our quality of life. There is a direct connection between the great composers of centuries past and the sounds we like today, no matter what genre, irrespective of the form.

Music imbues so many aspects of our lives. It affects the way we feel, enhances our self image, and solidifies our sense of community. The sounds of our lives go to the very core and touch our subconscious. Now, I realize that one man's melody might be noise to someone else. The definition of cacophony is not black and white. Some music is definitely an acquired taste.

I'm lucky to have been exposed to a broad range of sounds. I'd encourage you to try listening to something outside your preferred style. Who knows what you might learn to like? As someone once said, tomorrow is another day.

<u>44: Baseball</u>
July 8, 2008

In 1990, I attended the World Series in Oakland with a buddy of mine, Rich Palmer --
who is, by the way, a big supporter of the Fresno Grizzlies. We sat there, overlooking
the field, unaware that the A's were about to lose their third of four games in a row to
Cincinnati. Rich turned to me and said, "Terry, this is the great American spectacle." I
remember that. He didn't call it the national pastime as most people do, but the great
American spectacle.

You may consider the beauty of many other sports: tennis, cricket, golf. Nothing
compares with the one game which is truly unique to this country. Oh sure, there are
baseball diamonds all around the world from Canada to Japan to the Dominican
Republic. I've even seen baseball in Russia. It's not the same. For some reason, to be
authentic, baseball must be played in this land.

One great thing about watching the game is that it can be enjoyed as much by non-
athletes as by jocks. I was not much of a ball player as a kid. I couldn't throw very well,
couldn't catch, couldn't hit, couldn't run. No wonder, then, that I was cast as the Devil in
a community theater production of Damn Yankees.

Still, I always liked baseball. My father was Greek. Before coming to America, he had a
career as a soccer player. He never played baseball but he became a fan, too.

I occasionally criticize the amount of money devoted to athletics in this country. I hate
what some big companies have done to sports. I hated the 1994 baseball strike. The
players and the owners let greed get in the way of a great tradition.

We can continue to debate the economics of local sports, and their effect on our quality
of life. We certainly should have other priorities. But no one can question the feeling of
sitting out there in a ball park, having a hot dog and a soda or a beer and watching that
great American spectacle.

45: College Sports
January 2, 2007

There's no doubt that sports plays a huge role in the quality of our lives. That includes life on campus. We like to watch, we like to compete and we like to win.

It is impossible to eliminate money as an influence in sports. We can set all the rules we want. But as long as there's a profit to be made somewhere, big bucks will eventually have an effect. And the more money that's involved, the more difficult it is to resist its corrupting influence. On the other hand, that's true everywhere -- not just in athletics.

Scoring a lot of points is no substitute for academic accomplishment. An institution of higher learning is not just a venue for athletics. More than anything else, colleges and universities must educate their students -- all their students.

Let's get over the idea that jocks are dumb. Some of the smartest people I know are good athletes. And some of the stupidest can't toss a ball to save their lives. I agree with the ancient Greco-Roman virtue: *mens sana in corpore sano*, a sound mind within a sound body.

Having said that, I guess I can afford to lose a few pounds this year.

SCIENCE AND TECHNOLOGY

46: Moderation
March 27, 2007

The business card Valley Public Radio printed for me lists my title as moderator. I like to think of myself as a moderate person. I have lots of different opinions. I'm liberal about some things, conservative about others. Occasionally, I'm even radical. But on this program, my job is to be moderate. The role of moderator is to give a fair chance for all reasonable points of view.

Today, you heard competing sides of the global warming argument. So, are we humans pumping too much carbon dioxide into the atmosphere? As a result, is the greenhouse effect trapping the sun's rays and causing the earth's surface temperature to rise at a dangerous level? And because of this climate change, will the polar ice caps and arctic glaciers melt away? And ultimately, will all that lead to floods and other disasters?

Well, I'm not sure, but let me go out on a limb here and give you a personal opinion. Based on the preponderance of scientific evidence, I believe that the warnings about climate change probably are true -- and that we ought to do something. Fortunately, most of the things we can do are not bad.

Who can argue against being more frugal? Conserving our limited natural resources is simply logical. You remember the old saying, "Waste not; want not." Well, how about turning off the lights in the room when you're not using them? What's wrong with driving a fuel-efficient vehicle? Why shouldn't every new home built in the Central Valley have solar panels on the roof? And where's the downside to recycling?

Yes, it's possible that all those scientists are wrong. If they are, we'll end up with more energy and more money. But if they're right, we might just save our planet.

47: Reliability
July 15, 2008

Having worked for both a cable TV company and a wireless telecom service provider, I feel some personal responsibility for encouraging the public to adopt these devices before they were reliable. Compared to older technologies, some say cell phones, cable and satellite TV are still not ready for prime time. Not to mention computers.

Let me ask you a few questions. In a disaster, which would you prefer to have in your home?
1. A battery-operated cell phone that might work?
2. A computer-based phone system that requires both electricity and broadband?
3. An old-fashioned, rotary-dial telephone connected by copper wires to a reliable, independently powered network?

Of course, the answer is all three. And you'd probably want a satellite phone with solar panels and a generator back-up, too.

When it comes to TV, why do we need to pay for 500 channels when we really only watch five or ten? Especially when half the time they show infomercials? Of course, the answer is that it's more profitable. On the other hand, we probably couldn't afford to have only the channels we want anymore than we could afford to eat at a restaurant that served only the food we liked prepared only the way we preferred.

A free market economy requires both quantity and quality. I believe in regulated capitalism, the kind we had in the old Bell System days. As technology got more complicated, we let industry regulate itself. Unfortunately, the marketplace does not always determine whether products are good, or even good enough, only whether they are better or worse than their competitors.

Government regulation does not need to crush capitalism. Then again, free enterprise should not be free of responsibility. The very least we should require is that cell phones be as reliable as tin cans and string. Can you hear me now?

48: Climate Change
February 2, 2010

There are those who believe human beings have no responsibility for what's happening to the environment. Others argue that people are largely to blame for our ecological troubles. Some think the jury is still out, that we should wait for more evidence.

Here's my point of view. It really doesn't matter who or what is responsible. Whether you or I have caused something bad to happen is irrelevant. However, if we can mitigate the effects of catastrophic conditions, I think we should. Particularly if people will suffer by our inaction.

For example, after the earthquake struck Haiti a few weeks ago, some demagogic broadcasters like Pat Robertson and Rush Limbaugh exploited that human misery for their own gratification. The civilized world rushed to provide aid to the victims rather than stand pat and blame them. We could have done nothing. But helping Haitians was the right thing to do. The decent thing to do. And in the long run, it serves us all as human beings.

So it is with the problem of climate change. Scientists around the world have found compelling evidence that the planet's temperature is rising. We can see it for ourselves. The polar ice caps are melting. Weather conditions are crazier than ever before. Here in the west, forest fires are getting worse every year.

Now, could all this be part of a natural cycle? Perhaps. Could we say that curbing the amount of pollution which we put into our environment would cost too much money? Sure. But with what consequences? Save a few jobs today. Lose a lot of lives tomorrow. That sounds like a bad deal to me.

The fate of future generations is at stake. Possibly even our own. Responding to this impending crisis does not require an act of faith or an act of god. It just requires us to use our innate abilities and moderate our greed.

49: Nuclear Power
January 23, 2007

Comedian George Carlin once said, "A lot of the people who worry about the safety of nuclear power plants don't bother using their seat belts."

Now, I don't know if that's true, but I do know we have plenty of things to worry about. Nuclear energy is only one of them. We should be concerned about being too reliant on imported fuel. We should be concerned about using fuel that threatens our environment. We should be concerned about running out of fuel.

Sometimes, I wonder whether we're too greedy. Americans use far more energy than the rest of the world. The reality is that if we all just conserved a little bit, our consumption would diminish dramatically. Unfortunately, it's not in our national character to do with less. Maybe what we truly need is some encouragement.

Nothing motivates us more than money. So, what about a huge rebate for saving fuel? Suppliers of electricity and natural gas give consumers a price break for buying energy-efficient appliances. Why not require oil companies to do the same: offer big discounts for high-mileage vehicles?

I'd like to see gasoline hogs pay triple at the pump -- say, nine or ten bucks a gallon. And let's drop the price of unleaded back to fifty cents a gallon for anyone driving a less-wasteful car. That would get everybody's attention.

I know what you're thinking. This is a free-market economy. Our government should not control prices. Plus, it would be unfair to those who can't afford to buy fuel-efficient transportation. OK, then how about this? We keep hearing that America is at war. Fine. So, why aren't we rationing essential resources? If it was good enough for the greatest generation, it should be good enough for us, too.

Nuclear power might be a good idea, as long as we can be sure it's reasonably affordable and safe. I like mushrooms on my pizza, not in a cloud.

<u>50: Solving Problems</u>
May 13, 2008

The most fundamental principle of ethics is the golden rule. But you have to wonder how many people truly believe in doing unto others as they would have others do unto them. Many seem to prefer the more cynical version which says, "Do unto others before they do unto you."

I think you can judge a person's commitment to the golden rule by asking if he or she looks at the world as a zero-sum game. If so, that means there are winners and losers. If not, then it's possible for everyone to win.

It's hard to think about the big picture when there are so many catastrophes to deal with simultaneously. Climate change, war, natural disasters, poverty, disease, homelessness -- all of that can be overwhelming. My seventh grade math teacher, Tom Hodgdon, taught me how to solve complicated algebra problems by breaking them down into their simplest components. Figure out how to do the easy math, then apply that to the more complex puzzle. That actually works with all difficult problems: Start with the small things.

We might not be able to save the planet, but we can plant a tree or adopt an abandoned puppy. Don't know what to do about global warming? No problem. Just replace your incandescent light bulbs with CFLs and drive your car less often. The threat of terrorism got you down? Try meeting people who are different than you are, and listen to them. You'd be surprised how much alike we all are.

Of course, if you're interested in running for public office, that's good, too. But not all of us have to save the entire earth today. On the other hand, each of us can do something. I'd suggest that we all start by being a bit nicer to others. That sort of thing can be contagious!

51: True Conservatives
July 24, 2007

I love language. I think the words we use influence the way we think. Take the word "conservation" meaning to preserve, protect or keep the same. It's very close to the word "conservative." You might expect political conservatives and conservationists both would favor limiting human encroachment into nature. Well, you'd be wrong. In fact, there's a battle raging between those two ideologies.

Today, our focus is on water. It's one of our most precious natural resources, especially here in the Central Valley. Life as we know it would not exist but for our ability to import and manage water. But as with many other limited commodities, we compete against our neighbors for access to water. At the same time, given our traditional independent spirit, we want to use resources without outside interference. Whether it's water, plants, animals or even the land itself, we don't want anyone else to tell us what to do with our possessions.

But as we've come to learn, natural resources are not infinite. For the sake of our survival, for future generations, for our species, for the planet, we must exercise some responsibility. To put it bluntly, selfishness is suicidal. Fortunately, we do have the means to regulate our use of air and water and land. We can take steps to ensure the quality of life for everyone. All it takes is the will.

Whether we call ourselves conservatives or liberals, all of us should share at least one common goal: life.

POLITICS AND PUBLIC POLICY

52: Patriotism
July 3, 2007

Mark Twain's War Prayer ends with these words: "It was believed that the man was a lunatic, because there was no sense in what he said."

We've been talking today about patriotism, meaning support for one's country. That often translates into support for our troops. At this very moment, more than one hundred thousand Americans in uniform have taken up arms and are risking their lives overseas. Meanwhile, back at home, our first responders -- police officers, firefighters and others -- face daily dangers protecting us against a multitude of threats.

In one sense, we can say that it's all in defense of freedom, whether it be personal freedom or national freedom. But in a larger sense, it is part of the never-ending struggle for survival. More than 230 years ago, the War for Independence established an American tradition: our willingness to use force -- if necessary, deadly force -- in the name of liberty. Throughout human history, people have killed each other to achieve various goals: political, cultural, territorial. At this point in history, our species is engaged in myriad military conflicts. Iraq and Afghanistan are only two such places. There are at dozens of others around the planet, from Algeria to Zaire and from Columbia to Kashmir.

I would like to pose a philosophical question: Will we ever be able to solve our differences without violence? Or, must we accept the inevitability of war? I don't know. Maybe we'll get there someday. Until then, I guess the best we can do is hope. Oh, and if we're ever given a choice of whether to start another unnecessary war, we should probably just say, "No."

53: Growth
June 5, 2007

When I was a young lad back in 1961, my family moved from Fresno to San Jose. We bought a brand new, three-bedroom house in a nice neighborhood for $16,000. That same house today would sell for well over half a million bucks.

How the world has changed. Forty years ago, my father earned enough on middle class wages to support the family. My mom worked part-time because she wanted to, not because she had to.

Fresno was a rather sleepy town in the early sixties. The Bay Area was growing, but it was still possible to get around without terrible traffic problems. There was lots of open space. Gasoline cost about twenty-five cents a gallon.

I know: We can't back to those kinder, gentler days. Apart from my nostalgic feelings, the 1960s weren't exactly utopia, either. We had social upheaval and a little quagmire called the Vietnam War.

Today, life in the Central Valley is moving along at break-neck speed. OK, it's not New York City. But it isn't exactly Hicksville anymore, either. We face many of the same challenges as any big city in America: crime, air pollution, traffic congestion, and yes, housing.

One difference between small towns and big cities is population density. So, for example, mass transit is much more difficult to engineer in rural and suburban areas than in more crowded urban centers. For that reason, we Central Californians drive a lot, which means we spend more on gasoline. We also don't walk as much for which we pay in obesity.

Among the many things we can learn from history is how to manage the development of our cities. Of course, there's no realistic way to stop growth. But as in other aspects of our lives, I think we must consider the proposition that bigger is not necessarily better. That is as true of our homes and our communities as it is of our waistlines.

<u>54: Veterans Day</u>
May 29, 2007

This past weekend, we honored our fellow citizens who lost their lives in the nation's military service. For the past hour, we've been talking about the survivors of war. Now, let me put things in perspective concerning our present armed conflict.

A little more than four years ago, U.S. forces invaded Iraq. As of today
- At least 3,452 Americans are dead.
- More than 25,000 have been wounded in action.
- At least 7,000 others have received non-combat-related injuries.
- About 20,000 have left Iraq due to illness.
- Then there are non-military employees, so-called contractors. More than 900 killed and more than 12,000 wounded or injured.

In total, at least 68,000 American casualties killed, wounded, injured, or otherwise incapacitated. This does not include U.S. troops in Afghanistan. At last report, 390 deaths and nearly 6,000 non-fatal injuries.

It also does not count other coalition troops, let alone non-combatants. While our politicians debate what to do, the number of victims continues to rise.

Most people don't like to talk about Iraq. Those who support the present policy consider critical questions to be unpatriotic. Those who oppose the policy are frustrated. President Bush is quite correct about one thing: No matter what we do, things are going to get worse before they get better -- I would add, if they get better.

For the moment, the decision is clearly in the hands of the present administration. But this being a representative democracy, the final choice is in our hands. Come November of next year, we will choose a new President and some new members of Congress. By doing so, we will decide (among other things) whether we stay in Iraq or leave. Either way, we will have to live with the consequences of our country's actions: our choice, our responsibility.

Meanwhile, we will keep honoring our dead, treating our wounded, comforting their families, and hoping for the best.

55: Genocide
April 24, 2007

Last week, I ended the program by talking about indecency on the airwaves. Today, I want to say a word about a different kind of indecency: ignorance. I don't mean the lack of formal education. I'm referring to the intentional ignoring of inhumanity for which we are responsible.

In my previous commentary, I described the Fox New Channel as a perversion of journalism because they present an overtly partisan view. But to a lesser extent, the other mainstream media also fail to broadcast fair and balanced news reports. No matter what the networks do, however, we have an independent opportunity and the duty to find out what's happening in the world -- particularly what's being done in our name, with our money.

Last Tuesday was income tax day in the United States, the day we are obligated to contribute our fair share to the national treasury. Along with that duty, we should make sure our money is being spent wisely, morally, honestly. As citizens, we have the right and the responsibility to tell our government what to do for us. That includes protecting the innocent, both at home and abroad.

At the moment, we are directly responsible for the chaos caused by our invasions of Iraq and Afghanistan. We're also guilty of crimes by omission in Rwanda, Sudan, Nigeria, Senegal, Somalia, Sri Lanka, Colombia, Kashmir, the Ivory Coast, Abkhazia South Ossetia and Uganda. In every one of those countries, we are ignoring innocent victims of ongoing civil wars. We're doing nearly nothing to stop the horrors there.

Yes, I know: We can't solve all the world's conflicts. But we do seem quite capable of causing them. We have a long history of invading other nations, beginning with the native tribes on this continent. As with all injustices, we can't change the past. I do hope we will learn from it and embrace those two words, "never again."

56: Terrorism
September 11, 2007

This date has taken on a special meaning for us. It is inextricably connected with attacks on the World Trade Center and the Pentagon. It represents a turning point in our lives.

Throughout history, human beings have used violence or the threat of violence to achieve political goals. When it's done against us, we call it terrorism. When it's done by us, we call it freedom fighting.

Obviously, terror is nothing new. September 11th didn't change everything. It was a terrible event. But apart from the fact that flying is much less convenient today, the world and our country continue essentially unaltered.

And yet, we are told to be afraid. We are told that Americans must fight in a global war against terrorists. I know there are dangers at home and abroad. But I believe that we are not better off in conflict than in peace. We do not need to be afraid in order to be safe. Fear will not protect us. The way to fight danger is through understanding.

For my part, I've chosen to change the way I think and speak about war. To the best of my knowledge, the United States is not truly at war. Obviously, Americans are fighting in Iraq and Afghanistan. But that combat is not the same as war. There is no enemy state to oppose, no capital city to conquer, no leader to surrender, no concrete way for this engagement to be won or lost militarily.

The problem is that we accept the language, and therefore, the logic of war. This allows our authorities to justify many measures such as suspension of civil rights and the allocation of great resources, which we would quite possibly permit if it were actually a war.

I'm not so naïve as to think this situation will end easily if ever. But I'm just optimistic enough to believe we can make our world a little less terrible, less terrorized. It depends on those of us who are willing to reason together.

So, the next time someone tells you that we are fighting a war, don't be afraid. Just tell the truth: This may be a tragedy, but simply calling it a war does not make it so.

<u>57: State Initiatives</u>
January 22, 2008

Here in California, we've had the right to propose and vote on laws directly for almost a century. The intended purpose was to give citizens the power to prevent big money interests from corrupting the political process. We know how well that worked out.

Unfortunately, rather than preventing the super rich from controlling government, the current law makes it easier. What's worse, some initiatives are so complicated that almost no one can fully comprehend them. Another problem is that initiatives can show up on any ballot, not only during a general election. The problem is that during primaries or special elections, turn-out is typically quite low. So, a fraction of those eligible to vote can pass laws. Sounds a little un-democratic to me.

Well, I have a suggestion: Let's restore the initiative rules to their original form, the so-called "indirect initiative." Instead of politicians and their special interest groups proposing laws for us to vote on, we should have the right to propose legislation for our elected representatives to pass. After all, that is their job. And let's require propositions to be passed by a majority of registered voters -- not just a plurality of those who show up to vote.

Speaking of showing up, I hope you will. It might be a terrible way to govern, but at the moment, it's the only one we have. Besides, consider the alternative.

<u>58: Third Parties</u>
January 29, 2008

The President of the United States has one of the most unusual job descriptions in the world. There are very few absolute requirements. According to the Constitution, he or she must be a natural born citizen, be at least 35 years old, and not have been elected to this office more than once before.

That's not much to go on -- no minimum education, experience or references. No written exam, no physical or mental agility standards, not even an eye chart test. There are more requirements for getting a driver's license than for becoming commander in chief. No, that decision is simply left to us, the people.

So, what other qualifications do we look for in a president? Like most executives, this person should have leadership abilities. We would hope for good judgment, intelligence and pertinent knowledge. The job often requires communication skills, although that does not always mean eloquence. Some skills seem contradictory. At times, a president must be decisive. Then again, a president must be deliberative.

Other qualities include charisma, self-confidence, and that most elusive factor of all, the appearance of being presidential. There is one more trait that might be important in a president: having some active military experience. Most presidents have had some. It's difficult to appreciate the chain of command if you haven't been part of it.

Political campaigns are often messy and unpredictable events. All too often, they fail to do more than manipulate public opinion without enlightening anyone. However, these contests (if I may use that word) do provide some memorable ideas. The notion that most marks this current campaign is "change."

Prior to the 1992 presidential election, I was living and working in Russia. One day, I was at the U.S. embassy in Moscow and noticed a sign near one of their cash registers. It read, "We desperately need change." I presume they meant coins and small dollar bills.

Anyway, whoever is elected president, there is little doubt that America will change. But it probably won't be a drastic change. This country is like an aircraft carrier. No matter what the commander orders, movement is slow and gradual. Do we desperately need change? I don't know. I hope that whatever comes will be an improvement. Perhaps that's the best way to vote -- for someone better.

59: Party Politics
November 6, 2007

News agencies often compare political campaigns to horse races. We hear who's ahead or behind, why they're winning or losing. We often learn how much money they have or who supports them. Sometimes, we even get a glimpse of what they think about this issue or that issue as long as it's not too specific. Unfortunately, most of what we're hearing about those running for President is cosmetic. Who seems presidential? Who is too far to the left or the right? Who's made a gaffe?

Let's face it, politicians never want to say anything that will get them into trouble. But it's not entirely their fault. When they tell us the truth, especially if the truth is unpalatable, we reject them. When politicians say something unconventional, many voters get nervous and choose someone who sounds more moderate.

Of course, the information we want is exactly what they won't tell us: For example, the most important task a prospective President has, even before getting nominated, is choosing a vice-president and assembling a team to lead his or her administration. I want to know who those people will be before I cast my vote in the primaries.

Instead, between now and February 5, we will be seeing the world's longest and most expensive TV reality show. Who's leading in the polls? Who's catching up? Who will be voted off the island? I know there must be a better way to choose the next President of the United States.

<u>60: Why Vote?</u>
June 3, 2008

Yesterday I was talking with a young man who works at the hotel where I'm staying. He mentioned that he turned 18 last year and is old enough to vote now, but he doesn't know which political party to join. Most of his relatives are Republicans, but he's not sure that either party represents his own opinions.

I've heard similar views from Democrats. Surveys find one in three Americans consider themselves to be independent voters. A large percentage express disillusionment at the system and the candidates. In recent elections, many have complained about their lack of confidence in voting methods and in vote counting.

We often hear the phrase: "One person, one vote." But is that true? Some people are disenfranchised. Others feel their vote doesn't matter. Many simply don't bother to participate in elections.

Here's a thought: Rather than one person, one vote -- how about one person, ten votes? After all, during the primary election, votes are proportionately translated into delegates. And in the general election, votes are only symbolic since the President is really chosen by the Electoral College. So, why not give each of us multiple votes to divide among the various candidates, according to our preference?

Now, before you dismiss my idea as crazy, consider this: Big companies and rich individuals routinely give money to candidates from both major parties. They hedge their bets, thus guaranteeing access. Yet, when was the last time a member of Congress was prosecuted for being influenced by campaign contributions? Accepting money in exchange for a favor. That sure sounds a lot like the definition of bribery. And you say I'm crazy?!

61: Counting Votes
October 12, 2010

From time to time, I hear people say their vote doesn't matter. And I can see why one might feel that way. Out of millions of votes, what difference does one ballot make? Usually, not much.

But in a mid-term, the total number of votes is typically smaller. So statistically, each vote is more significant. And sometimes, elections are won by a single vote.

Thomas Jefferson was elected President by one vote in the U.S. House of Representatives. Andrew Jackson lost by the same number. Andrew Johnson was impeached but remained President because one senator voted against conviction. And Texas became a state by the vote of one senator.

But wait, I hear you say. That was way back in the 1800s. How about something a bit more current? OK. In the 1990s, governors in Maine, Rhode Island, Alaska and North Dakota all got elected by one vote per precinct. Members of Congress from several states have recently been elected with a similar majority.

Want something closer to home? Two years ago, a Stockton Unified School trustee was elected by one vote. All this to say that your participation is important. Now maybe you don't like the system. I'm not all that crazy about it myself. The process could certainly benefit from some improvements. But until we make it better, I guess we'll have to continue exercising the power in our hands.

I just wish running for office didn't cost so much money.

Today, we've been talking about politics and mental health care. A cynical person might say that there's a connection between these two topics. And maybe there is. Call me crazy, but I think our system of governance has become a bit dysfunctional.

Take the initiative process. It was originally meant for citizens to overcome a corrupt legislature. Ironically, these days it is often legislators themselves who propose laws in this way. And, of course, big businesses, labor unions and other powerful groups. For about a million dollars, practically anyone can hire professionals to gather the necessary number of signatures and get almost any proposition they want on the state ballot.

And what's wrong with that? Well first, this process is contrary to the very notion of representative democracy. Second, there's little or no chance to debate these propositions, let alone amend them. It's just take it or leave it. Third, and perhaps worst of all, initiatives can have unintended consequences that make matters even worse and with no good solutions.

The result is a confusing collection of constitutional and regulatory provisions unfathomable to mortal men and women. Yet every time someone has an issue or a cause unsatisfied by the regular lawmaking process, we get to vote on another set of complicated propositions. And when that fails, we do it again and again.

Now, I'm no doctor, but these symptoms seem to indicate that our body politic is in need of professional help. Unfortunately, the help we usually get is from consultants and lobbyists and politicians. That would be like sending a lung cancer patient to the tobacco companies for treatment. Smoke two packs and call me in the morning.

So, what can we do? How about a moratorium on propositions? The next time someone asks you to sign a petition, read it first. Ask the petitioner how much he or she is getting paid to promote that initiative and why it should be passed. If you don't get reasonable answers, just say no.

Then, maybe our elected representatives will do their jobs. And if they don't, we should fire them at the next election. After all, isn't that the way a democracy is supposed to work?

<u>63: Electoral Reform</u>
January 5, 2010

As happy as we might be with our system of government, there's always room for improvement. The question is how to make things better.

I've long been opposed to fast, violent changes. Sometimes, a quick and powerful response appears to be necessary, even unavoidable. However, the use of lethal force to achieve long-term social and political goals is almost never a good idea.

During the late 1980s and 90s, I witnessed some rather dramatic transformations in Europe and the former Soviet Union. The Berlin Wall fell down and other dominoes came tumbling after. It was an era marked by dozens of revolutions -- some peaceful, others, not so much. Twenty years later, life in those countries is quite different. They have more participatory governments and relatively free-market economies.

Many people have taken advantage of new opportunities and live much better today. Millions of others are worse off -- victims of organized crime, corruption, political instability and the economic roller coaster that typifies our new world order.

Or is it the new world disorder? Sometimes, I'm not so sure. What I do know is this: Radical changes often have unpredictable consequences. The American Revolution gave us our Bill of Rights and hate speech. The Wright Brothers enabled air travel and air sickness. Albert Einstein opened the door to nuclear power and nuclear weapons. All that doesn't mean change is a bad thing. But as the old saying goes, "Be careful what you wish for because you just might get it."

64: Free Speech
March 9, 2010

Thomas Jefferson also championed the right of expression. To paraphrase our third President, a democracy cannot be both free and ignorant. My fear is that we are tilting dangerously toward the latter and away from the former.

For speech to be free, it must also be informed. Merely making noise does not advance the quality of life. That's why people aren't supposed to lie. There's a difference between patriotism and propaganda. We should be wary of hypocrisy. No matter how foxy it sounds. No matter how much of a rush we're in. No matter who beckons. Puns definitely intended.

This does not only apply to media. Honesty should be the first rule of communication everywhere. Unfortunately, not everyone likes to hear the truth. And not everyone feels free to speak his or her mind. As we know, the First Amendment only guarantees us the right against government censorship. So, who protects content in other cases?

Individuals and institutions are understandably self-interested. Politicians and political parties want to protect their power. Businesses and executives want to protect their profits. Academia? Well, there's this little thing called tenure.

But all those interests should be balanced against the desire for personal expression. I believe the key here is reasonableness. It's easy to support only speech with which we agree. To listen only to those with whom we sympathize. To talk whenever and wherever the mood strikes us.

However, to make this so-called democracy work, we are obligated to respect the rights of others, too. We must also provide a fair hearing for our opponents. It's one thing to denounce liars. It's quite another to shout down honest differences. That's not dialogue. It's demagoguery.

My humble advice is this: Go out of your way to seek and truly consider a point of view that differs from your own. Who knows what truths you'll find among the fairytales.

65: Who Really Rules?
May 25, 2010

Whenever there's an election, I wonder about our so-called two party system. I say "so-called" because, in fact, we do have other parties. But it's very rare for a third-party candidate to be elected. Why is that?

Well, strictly speaking, we can vote for anyone who is qualified to hold office. But the Democrats and the Republicans have a virtual lock on our government. These days, there's a resurgence of interest in political change. That was in evidence two years ago. We also saw it across the Atlantic when Britain recently formed a coalition government. On the other hand, many voters express disappointment in their elected officials no matter which party they belong to.

Which begs the question, "Who really rules?" It's hardly a representative democracy when the same small group of politicians and their financial backers win every time. It's hardly even an election when some candidates run un-opposed such as right here in the Central Valley.

That issue came up last week, during a forum I attended at California State University in Bakersfield, sponsored by the Kegley Institute of Ethics and the Kern County Press Club. Their formal topic was the future of journalism ethics. But the panel also discussed the impact of journalism on government.

Nearly a century ago, the writer Humbert Wolfe wrote this mocking rhyme about reporters in England: "You cannot hope to bribe or twist, thank God, the British journalist. But seeing what the man will do unbribed, there's no occasion to."

I think it applies equally to my colleagues in this country. We have a lot of good and honest news reporters at NPR as well as at many local and national media companies. Unfortunately, there's also a lot of mediocrity and propaganda.

Part of our job as citizens is to determine what is true. That requires time and effort. But we risk losing our freedoms if we fail to educate ourselves. We can't choose our representatives when we don't know what the facts are. Here's my unsolicited bit of advice for today: While we still have the opportunity to do so, let's be good news consumers. I believe our quality of life, our very way of life depends on it.

<u>66: Political Advertising</u>
October 5, 2010

Some years ago, I heard the general manager of another radio station speaking about the "funny voices" we hear on the air from time to time -- voices saying things like "Paid for by Jones for dog catcher" or "I'm Willy Wilson and I approved this message." It's a ridiculous by-product of the federal law requiring a discount for candidates who appear in their own political ads.

Although the voices might be funny, their messages are quite serious and sometimes rather disturbing. Many people dread the onslaught of partisan publicity, promoting a pack of political competitors. Even worse is the fact that these would-be public servants must spend so much of their time raising money, most of it to cover the cost of messages on radio and TV. Candidates appeal to campaign contributors who effectively purchase access and influence by paying for those costly ads. This practice is an obvious corruption of our democracy.

Now, I understand. Broadcasters, particularly commercial broadcasters, have to earn a living by selling their air time. Some stations such as this one occasionally offer unpaid time for political announcements. But it's not enough.

I'd like to see all legitimate candidates given equal access to mass media during the run-up to elections free of charge, so office seekers can communicate with the electorate and not need to sell their souls to the highest bidder.

Last time I checked, the public airwaves still belonged to the public. So, let's require every station, radio and TV, commercial and non-commercial, cable, satellite, Internet, you name it -- all of them -- to operate in the public interest and put an end to paid political advertising. It'll be good for voters, good for candidates, good for government, and it might just silence all those funny voices.

Oh, by the way, I'm Terry Phillips and I approved this message.

<u>67: Predicting Votes</u>
October 26, 2010

Well, we're down to the last week before Election Day.

The subject of electoral reform is critically important to our democracy. Several of the initiatives on next week's ballot deal with that topic. We'll spend more time in the coming months talking about the process of governance.

For months, you've been hearing a lot of predictions about the likely outcome of these midterms. I always find such virtual horse races to be somewhat disturbing.

On one hand, it's understandable. We in the media are curious to know what will happen. So, we ask surveyors to find out, then pass on that information to you.

On the other hand, it strikes me as somewhat irresponsible to tell voters in advance how we will be voting. It's as if the decision has already been made, so why should we bother to cast our ballots? I'm as guilty as anyone else for doing this. Still, I wish these pre-election polls would not be published.

A couple years ago, we debated the question of whether voting should be compulsory. Several dozen countries require citizens to participate in elections. Failure can result in fines although relatively few enforce those laws.

Instead of mandating the vote, maybe we should start paying people to participate. Perhaps offer a tax break or free car washes or something. What would it take to get you to do your duty?

On our last program, a listener referred to this quotation: "Just because you do not take an interest in politics doesn't mean politics won't take an interest in you." That is attributed to the Greek orator Pericles in the year 430 B.C.

No matter what you think about government and politics, keep one more thing in mind. On November 2, someone is going to mark a ballot in exactly the opposite way that you would. You have the power to cancel out that other vote. On the other hand, your ballot could put some candidate or measure over the top and guarantee a victory. Either way, please vote. California needs all the help it can get.

November 13, 2007

One of the most difficult things to say is "I don't know." Whether you're a politician, a priest, a college student or a news reporter, ignorance is never a good option.

We have an almost instinctive desire to know things, to have solid answers to all our questions. Perhaps of equal importance, we want to know the truth. And the bigger the question, the greater our need to know.

At the same time, we prefer our truths to be black and white. Nuanced reality is uncomfortable, unsatisfying. After every prominent event in the era of modern communication, we expect our leaders to give us the answers, to tell us the truth.

But sometimes, our leaders lie. Sometimes, the truth is too elusive for us to validate. Sometimes, we want to throw our hands in the air and say, "We just don't know." What I do know is that it's better to rely on evidence and reason than on fear or fantasy.

I chose the topic of today's program because a listener sent me a copy of two books edited by our first guest, retired theology professor David Griffin. At the beginning of this hour, we heard him say the 9-11 attacks were orchestrated by officials of the American government. He suggests the Twin Towers were brought down by explosive charges, and not by fire following aircraft collisions. He says it was an inside job.

We then heard from Gene Corley, the leading independent engineer who examined the wreckage of that tragic event. His expertise and first-hand investigation led to an almost-universally accepted scientific conclusion. There is no credible evidence that the World Trade Center buildings were brought down by anything other than the physical forces subsequent to those airplane collisions.

Now, you might wonder as I have whether there is any truth to the alternative theories. I'll leave you to form your own opinion. But it seems to me the proof is quite clear. Of course, it's always good to keep an open mind. Because despite the old saying, nothing is certain -- not even death or taxes.

<u>69: Supporting the Troops</u>
June 12, 2006

You might say that nothing has changed. Since the beginning of recorded history, we have often resorted to military force as a means of settling our differences. Apparently, that's just the nature of being human. On the other hand, we Americans have a powerful sense of right and wrong. Being right is very important to us, even if we're not always seen as doing right.

We need to remember that war affects not only "our" troops and "their" troops and so-called "collateral" victims. It also affects the loved ones left behind. But what about the rest of us? For the most part, the fact is that our lives go on pretty as usual. Most of us are giving up nothing while our fellow countrymen are engaged in armed conflict.

And what can we do? The War on Terror requires no rationing, no blackouts, no tangible personal costs on the home front. Well, we can start by helping the families who have been deprived of a son or daughter, mother or father, husband or wife. Try to imagine what it would be like to have a loved one far away, in constant danger. Then think about how you'd want to be treated and act accordingly. For example, are there children in your community with parents in the military? Maybe you could include them in some of your own family activities. Most importantly, be a good friend.

No matter what our political views, whether we want U.S. forces in battle or not, they are there. It's high time we stop asking our fellow citizens to make great sacrifices unless we are willing to do so, too.

As we have heard today, appearance is important to everyone. It affects our personal relationships, our professional success, even the way we choose our political leaders.

In about three weeks, Russians will elect their next president. While living in Moscow, I discovered something called the theory of alternate succession. Over the past century, Kremlin rulers have gone back and forth from having hair on top of their heads to being rather bald. Czar Nicholas II had a full head of hair. Vladimir Lenin did not. Stalin had hair. Khrushchev had none. And so on and so forth through to Gorbachev with his famously smooth scalp, Yeltsin with lots of hair, Putin with relatively little, and his hair— I'm sorry, I mean his heir apparent, Dmitry Medvedev. He's very hairy.

We have no hirsute parallel to the Russian theory of alternate succession. There is a variation, of course. The American presidency might be passed from a Bush to a Clinton again. The outcome of today's primary elections will shed some light on that possibility.

No matter whom the Democrats and Republicans nominate, the next U.S. President will exercise some change and some continuity. The best we can hope for is that he or she will be smart enough to know which is best. For now, I'd suggest that you brush up on your relaxation techniques. Because the next nine months are going to feel like one long rhetorical rollercoaster ride.

Finally, let me say that we have all been disappointed by the poor quality of presidential candidates. But when you consider how inhumane the process is for getting that job, it's no wonder so few good people try. And once elected, the president is so vilified that you might think the only person who really loves him is his mother.

71: Colors
June 5, 2006

I'm convinced that there are no red states and blue states. People are not simply liberal or conservative, Republicans Democrats, Greens and all the rest. Such labels do not define you and me. They are simply convenient shorthand for those who want to manipulate us in furtherance of their own purposes.

On the other hand, we need to be smart enough to avoid getting trapped by such labels. Otherwise, we lose the very essence of democracy, the freedom to choose. Our government may be of the people, by the people and for the people, but unless we're careful, P.T. Barnum could turn out to be wrong. Perhaps you can fool all the people all the time.

<u>72: Pets</u>
May 8, 2007

Are you a dog person or a cat person? Rumor has it that you can tell a lot about someone by the kind of pet he or she likes. They say that dog people tend to be more sociable. Cat people are more independent. Canine lovers are more generous and helpful. Feline fanciers are more finicky and non-conformist. Dog owners watch TV. Cat owners read books. And all of this is poppycock. For example, what about people who have both cats and dogs?

On the other hand, I think there is a difference between those who love animals and those who don't. Generally speaking, pet owners are nicer people. They're also happier and healthier. According to medical experts, pets can lower our stress level, blood pressure, cholesterol and triglycerides. There is even a statistical correlation between pet ownership and longevity.

A dog or cat can be a fine judge of character. You can tell a lot about someone by the way his or her pet treats the owner. So, here's an idea that might help us decide who should be the next President of the United States.

Let's give each of the candidates a dog or a cat to take care of for one month. They must do no campaigning for thirty days. Just take care of that pet. At the end of those four weeks, we'll send in a team of animal psychologists to take away the cats and dogs, and return them to their original owners. If any one of them wants to stay with the politician, that person gets to be President. In case no human wins, we could let the animals run the country. They couldn't do any worse.

FOREIGN AND DOMESTIC

73: Immigration
October 12, 2005

Everyone came here from somewhere else. Many of us were born in another state, some in another country. All of us had immigrant parents or grandparents or some ancestors in our family. According to anthropologists, even native Americans migrated to this continent long ago. Maybe it's time for us to get over the idea that we belong here exclusively, that we have some unique birthright.

Maybe it's time to get over the idea that some people do not belong here. Apart from individuals who commit serious crimes, nobody deserves to be banished from any land.

The United States was created for the sake of liberty. Our forefathers (and foremothers) gave us political freedom, economic freedom, religious freedom. Do we now have the right to deny this freedom for future Americans?

On the other hand, our country has become much more populated -- and much more complicated. Complex problems require creative solutions and compromise. We need to regulate limited resources while keeping up with social changes. Immigrants should be able to preserve personal cultural identity, but must make an effort to assimilate into public life. That means learning the common language, participating in the political system, and obeying the law.

A colleague of mine, Shepard Sherbell, is a photojournalist. He was born in the United States. I met Shepard in Czechoslovakia just after the Velvet Revolution. When I asked him specifically where he was from, Shep answered, "As of now I'm from here."

Sounds right to me.

74: Common Values
February 20, 2007

I'm always fascinated by the concept of "us and them." In many ways -- in fact, in most ways -- all of us are almost exactly alike. And yet, we keep drawing lines of separation: for race, for gender, religion and of course, legal residency. We distinguish between those of us who were born here or who came here by law, versus those who are here without legal permission.

It seems rather hypocritical to me. We rely heavily on low-paid, undocumented, immigrant workers to harvest our food, build our neighborhoods, tend our gardens, clean our homes and our offices. At the same time, we vilify their illegal status while ignoring their inhumane living conditions. They frequently pay a high price just to get here. Many are here in hopes of finding a better life for themselves and their families. Some are here out of desperation, far away from their families.

Does this sound familiar? It should: It's the classic story of American immigrants, legal or otherwise. I bet you'll find such examples among your own ancestors.

Since this is Black History Month, let me quote Dr. Martin Luther King. He said, "Injustice anywhere is a threat to justice everywhere."

I believe justice means letting all those who come here have the same chance our Founding Fathers had -- none of whom, by the way, immigrated legally. Specifically, I think it's time for us to stop treating immigrants as criminals. We should give our fellow human beings the same welcome we would expect, and pay them the money they earn for the hard work that they do.

Oh, I know: Improving the lives of immigrants would cost a lot. On the other hand, think of how much we could save in law enforcement, health care, education -- and most important, humanity. I'd like to believe that is a value we all share.

The 1963 film "America, America" by Elia Kazan was based on the director's best-selling novel by the same name. If you've never seen the movie, I highly recommend it. Simply put, it's the story of an immigrant seeking the American dream. Let me tell you another such story.

Grigorios Phillipidis was an ethnic Greek born in Turkey -- just as in Kazan's movie. He also dreamed of coming to America. In 1948, as a merchant seaman, Grigorios landed on the East Coast, got shore leave, but never went back to his ship. Some years later, wishing to become a U-S citizen, he voluntarily left this country and returned legitimately. Then, as many immigrants did in those days, Grigorios Phillipidis Americanized his name to Greg Phillips.

As you might have guessed, this man was my father and yes, he originally came here an illegal alien. Although Dad never forgot his Greek roots, he was one of the most patriotic Americans I ever knew. I, myself, have been an illegal alien. As a foreign correspondent, I've crossed a number of borders without official permission. In fact, I did it again just last year while reporting a story in the former Soviet Union.

Now, some might speculate that this habit runs in my family. I'd say it goes even further. Crossing borders is a genetic trait of the human family. It is our nature to travel, with or without papers. But as our world has become more complicated, perceived threats to security have led to more barriers. I understand that people are afraid. We fear losing our jobs and even our lives from some foreign threat. But most of the harm done in this country is by people who are born here, not invaders from another land.

One of the greatest ways to overcome fear is through familiarity. Ignorance continues to fuel our irrational views of others. Relatively few Americans travel abroad. Some say it's because the United States is so vast that we don't need to go anywhere else for tourism or business.

That's a real pity. The world is full of fascinating people and places. Bearers of U.S. passports can enter many countries with no visa requirements. The wonders of modern communication and the globalized economy have made crossing borders a bit less magical than in centuries past. But that first time can still be memorable. And every time is full of possibilities.

The road always calls me. In my home office, I have a world map dotted with little colored push pins. The red pins indicate countries I've already visited. The blue ones mark future destinations. I'm a very lucky guy to have seen so much of this planet. And yet, there is so much more to see. I close with this thought: Go somewhere. Meet someone new. Learn to see your own world from a different point of view. But beware: travel can be addictive. You might even want to become an illegal alien.

76: My Brother's Keeper
September 15, 2009

While trying to think of a commentary for today, I was reminded that homelessness is very closely related to health care. Let's face it: Those who cannot afford to keep a roof over their heads are also among the most likely to need medical treatment. They also probably need help paying for doctors and hospitals and drugs.

Poor people tend to rely more on emergency rooms rather than seek preventive care. They often have compromised immune systems. They often have poor nutrition. The working poor often have dangerous employment and have a greater risk of on-the-job injuries. In brief, those with the fewest financial resources have the greatest need for public health care.

For the past few months, we've been wasting a lot of time hearing silly arguments about socialism and government intrusion into our personal rights. Those who make such baseless claims seem to be avoiding a fundamental question: What is our responsibility as a society to our fellow human beings?

In my view, the way you respond says a lot about your sense of decency. If you think we owe each other a helping hand whenever possible, in my view, that makes you a good person.

On the other hand, if you think others should live or die based on their own resources, that puts you in league with the murderer of Eden. According to the Genesis story, when Cain killed Abel, God asked him what happened. Cain answered, "Am I my brother's keeper?"

Now, I'm no biblical scholar. But it seems to me that those who oppose universal health care should just get out of the garden. Wouldn't it be better to work together and try to make this a better country for everyone? That might not lead us to paradise, but it sure beats the alternative.

<u>77: Big Cities</u>
September 25, 2007

I suppose we all dream about places where we'd rather be. At one time or another, almost every periodical has published a list of the best places to live in America.

This year, Money magazine says its top pick because of a booming economy, good schools, low crime and lots of green space is Middleton, Wisconsin.

According to Forbes magazine, the safest city in the United States is Honolulu, Hawaii. In case you're wondering, Forbes says the least safe is Monroe, Louisiana.

And the priciest city in America? That would be New York, where a penthouse in the Trump building will cost you a cool $70,000 a month.

Apart from expenses, our standard of living is affected by earning potential as well as total resources. But, of course, the quality of life also includes a lot of intangibles like cultural diversity, friendliness, even image. I know people in Manhattan who would rather die than live in California, or even west of the Hudson River. Then again, King Kong never climbed the Bakersfield sign or the Security Bank building.

My point is that while there might not be many skyscrapers around here, no one ever got hurt tripping over a giant ape carcass on the sidewalk, either.

<u>78: Small Towns</u>
October 2, 2007

How do we decide which is best: big cities or small towns? The other day, I was talking with my sister, Genese, about humor. She told me that a particular joke was not funny. I said it was. The truth is that if a joke makes someone laugh, it is funny to that person.

I think the same can be said about where we live. If you don't like the pace of life, the density, the climate or the overall character of a particular city or town, then you're probably better off living somewhere else.

There are some things we can all agree on. No matter where we live, the quality of life is also related to a number of intangibles such as dignity, well-being, happiness. I'm not sure those are determined by location as much as by fundamental humanity. Moreover, I am convinced that anyplace on earth can be the right place to live if your heart is there.

79: Bakersfield vs. Fresno
November 18, 2008

Today we debated the respective merits of the Central Valley's two largest cities, Fresno and Bakersfield. My friends in the Bay Area often tease me for having moved back here from Northern California. I spent much of the past week in the environs of San Francisco. That sainted city certainly has its own charm. How can we compete with Fisherman's Wharf and Coit Tower and the Golden Gate Bridge?

Then again, how can they compete with the down-to-earth life that comes from this garden that feeds the whole country? Yes, our air quality leaves something to be desired. Yes, we have no ocean breezes to cool off our triple-digit summer temperatures. And yes, we do not climb halfway to the stars in little cable cars. But the Central Valley has produced some of the most prolific writers and actors and athletes and entrepreneurs in the world.

Unlike our friends living that City by the Bay, there's no affectation about Fresno nor any pretentiousness about Bakersfield, nothing at all haughty about the dozens of small towns that dot this region. Our noses are not pointed up. They aim straight ahead.

Here in the Central Valley (to quote Flip Wilson's alter ego, Geraldine), "Honey, what you see is what you get." And may I add, that ain't all bad. It might not be the most politically progressive place on Earth nor the most socially avant-garde. In fact, you're unlikely to hear anyone even say "avant-garde" around these parts. What you will hear is, "Welcome, neighbor. How're you doing? And can I help you?" In the days and months ahead, that small-town attitude might turn out to be far more valuable than all the snooty restaurants from North Beach to Chinatown.

Don't get me wrong: I love San Francisco. Always have and always will. But if home is defined by the location of one's heart, with apologies to Tony Bennett, I left mine in Bakersfield.

80: Allensworth
April 15, 2008

For the past hour, we've been marking some great anniversaries. Columnist Frank Pelatowski is one hundred years old. The town of Allensworth is celebrating its centenary, too. This is also an anniversary for some famous African-Americans.

On this date in 1922, Harold Washington was born. You might remember him as the first black mayor of Chicago.

It's also the birthday in 1928 of Norma Merrick Sklarek, the first black female architect in California. And it was on April 15, 1947 that Jackie Robinson made his debut as the first black major league baseball player.

When it comes to African-Americans, we often recognizes firsts.

- Ralph Bunche became the first African American to win a Nobel Peace Prize in 1950.
- Forty years later, in 1990, Douglas Wilder of Virginia was elected the first black governor in the United States.
- Thurgood Marshall was the first African-American on the U.S. Supreme Court.
- Colin Powell was the first African-American to serve as Secretary of State.
- Max Robinson was the first African-American network anchorman.
- And Tiger Woods, whose father is black and whose mother is Thai, became both the first African-American and the first Asian-American to win the Masters golf tournament.

So, what does all this mean? It means that we may have come a long way, baby, but we still have a long way to go. These mileposts are evidence of progress. But the very fact that we continue to mark them is evidence we are not there yet. I say "we" because as long as we think of African-Americans or Asian-Americans or Latino-Americans as different or special or as others, we are not yet us.

81: Race Relations
April 22, 2008

Last week, we spent the hour learning about Allensworth. That Central Valley town was founded one hundred years ago by African-Americans and for African-Americans.

I asked our guests whether being racially separated was a contributing factor to the demise of Allensworth. The expert consensus was that racism, not voluntary segregation, was the root problem. By banding together, the black residents of Allensworth tried to prove that they could govern themselves successfully.

That experiment began a little more than forty years after the end of slavery in the United States. The battle for political, economic and social freedom was all uphill back then and it continues even now.

Today, we've been talking about race in twenty-first century America. Such words as Caucasian, Negro and Oriental are not only considered impolitic today. They are increasingly inaccurate.

Jim Crow laws have been wiped off the books. Integration is so commonplace we usually don't even refer to it anymore. Perhaps only those who lived through the Civil Rights era can fully see and understand the achievements of the past forty or fifty years.

And yet. And yet.

Yes, Barack Obama could well be elected President this year.

Yes, the second largest city in America has a Latino mayor.

Yes, many of our largest corporations are run by Asian-Americans.

But the very fact that these are still exceptional leads me to conclude the playing field is far from level. Compared to all other countries on earth, the United States remains unique as a land of opportunity. Nevertheless, we must keep pushing forward if the words in our nation's founding documents will ever become true. Are we all created equal? Of course not. Can we give each person an equal chance to achieve his or her own dreams? I hope so -- someday.

82: Culture Clashes
September 7, 2010

Today we've been talking about cultural diversity. We have a rich mixture of different nationalities here in the Central Valley. My own family includes elements of Greek, Armenian, Turkish, Egyptian, Brazilian and other influences. I'm lucky to be the son of multilingual parents who encouraged me to learn the common language of this country while never forgetting our ancestral origins.

Words are very important to me. I strongly believe that our most serious problems are rooted in miscommunication. What we say does not always correspondent to what we think. More often than not, I believe we would agree with each other if we only spoke honestly. Take the two classic controversies: religion and politics.

As we approach the November elections, political opponents are trying to convince us, as usual, that we have fundamental differences of left and right, this party or that one, my candidate or yours. But when you come right down to it, we all want essentially the same things: physical security, economic stability, personal freedom and so on.

As for religion, we often confuse the words belief and knowledge. Despite all evidence to the contrary, a shockingly large number of Americans still mistakenly believe Barack Obama is a Muslim.

Many people think that facts are incompatible with faith. Even the idea of God is often expressed unclearly. Our attitudes tend to be molded by the words we use to describe deity. Maybe fewer people would call themselves atheists if they knew what the word "God" meant.

This week marks the end of Ramadan and the beginning of Rosh Hashanah. A few weeks ago, I spoke with Kamal Abu-Shamsieh, Director of the Islamic Cultural Center in Fresno. He told me about the increase of prejudice directed against Muslims here in the Central Valley. That's odd in a place where so many people claim to believe in brotherhood.

Our diversity is supposed to make us stronger. And yet, we have so many different belief systems. Maybe that's why it is difficult to remember our common values. Instead, we get caught in pointless arguments about contrary positions. There's nothing wrong with a good debate as long as it leads to a better world. At least that's what I'd like to imagine.

<u>83: Travels</u>
March 13, 2007

One of my favorite movie quotes is from "The Adventures of Buckaroo Banzai Across the 8th Dimension." The main character says, "No matter where you go, there you are."

I love to travel. Nothing makes me happier than going somewhere. Part of it, I suppose, is the sense of adventure. Part of it is my desire to escape. But I've never managed to get away from myself. No matter where I go, I'm still there. I guess Buckaroo was right.

On the other hand, travel has certainly given me a wonderful sense of perspective, a greater appreciation for my country and our connection to the world. I think it's sad that most Americans never travel outside the United States. I know that it can be expensive to go abroad -- even to go from coast to coast. This is a big country.

Nevertheless, there is nothing that compares with the experiences one gains while on the road. I guess if I were king, I would require every citizen to spend at least some time outside the realm. I'm not talking about the kind of insular travel many of us prefer. Not a Club Med vacation. I mean having contact with other people in other lands, getting to know them the way they live, discovering what they think and how they feel.

I'm just optimistic enough to believe the world would be a better place if we all got to know each other. Most of us know very little about the rest of the world. By contrast, the rest of the world knows us quite well.

Some people want us to think that we are hated by those in other countries. Having been to some of those other countries myself, I can assure you that most of them like us. They admire and envy our way of life. They watch our movies, listen to our music, buy our soft drinks, and wear our jeans. They imitate our ideals, even if we don't always practice them ourselves. The rest of the world is much more American than you might think.

As I see it, people in other countries don't hate us because of what they know; we fear them because of what we don't know. Isn't it time we corrected that mistake?

Note: In retrospect, I should have quoted Mark Twain: "Travel is fatal to prejudice, bigotry, and narrow-mindedness, and many of our people need it sorely on these accounts. Broad, wholesome, charitable views of men and things cannot be acquired by vegetating in one little corner of the earth all one's lifetime." (*Innocents Abroad*)

LAW AND ORDER

84: Gangs
October 26, 2005

Everybody wants to fit in somewhere, kids and grownups alike. A lot of young people join gangs to have somewhere to go and something to do. Gangs are surrogate families.

But we human beings are also creatures of conflict. Unfortunately, a lot of gang members break the law. No matter what else they might be, many gangsters are connected with organized crime.

Now, violence is not a good way to resolve conflict. It's neither romantic nor honorable. Violent crimes produce real victims. To protect ourselves from further harm and to punish lawbreakers, we understandably incarcerate those who commit felonies. At the same time, imprisoning people does not remove the root causes of violence.

Our criminal justice system deals primarily with the aftermath of crime. Most police and prosecutors do their best but they're far from perfect. Sometimes they are even part of the problem. Where we have failed most is in crime prevention. That begins at home and at school and at work.

It's relatively easy not to commit violent crimes when life is good. But desperation often leads to bad choices. The bottom line is this: If we want to live in a safer society, life needs to be better for everyone.

As the writer H.L. Mencken once said, "There is always an easy solution to every human problem -- neat, plausible and wrong." [Note: This was from "The Divine Afflatus" and was published in the *New York Evening Mail* on November 16, 1917.]

May 22, 2007

I grew up in an era when Westerns dominated popular entertainment. One of my heroes was the cowboy character, Hopalong Cassidy. Here in the Central Valley, his face was on every carton of Producer's Dairy milk. I watched Hoppy on TV all the time. When I was about five years old, the thrill of my young life was meeting William Boyd, the actor who played that role. It was at a public appearance here in Fresno. He wore his cowboy clothes, I wore mine, and we each had a six-shooter.

Like most little boys in those days, I played war games, cops and robbers, cowboys and Indians. It's no surprise, then, that I developed a romanticized appreciation for guns. I've also enjoyed shooting them. They are amazing, fascinating devices. They are a source of power. Millions of people use firearms legally and safely: hunters, target shooters, collectors. Guns can protect lives. They can also take lives.

It really wasn't until I worked as a news reporter and saw firearms used in combat that I fully understood how dangerous they were. I felt awful the first time I saw the victim of a gunshot wound. I'm not sure how many lives would be saved or lost without guns. There's probably no way to know.

As with so many other problems, we tend to treat the symptoms more than the causes. To stop people from abusing firearms, we need to stop human violence. So many complex factors are at the root of violence, such as poverty and mental illness. But our own attitude is also a factor.

Do you remember Gene Autry's Cowboy Code? It included such things as:
- The cowboy must never shoot first, hit a smaller man, or take unfair advantage.
- He must always tell the truth and help people in distress.

Contrary to the modern maverick image of a cowboy who never avoids a fight, Gene Autry's code encourages us to act responsibly. That attitude has made us part of the problem, both at home and around the world. Stopping violence begins with each of us. Maybe, just maybe by following this cowboy code, maybe we can lower the rate of violence and improve everyone's quality of life.

86: Prisons
August 21, 2007

As near as I can tell, we have prisons for several reasons. First, we want to keep safe from those who would do us harm. Second, we have prisons to persuade people not to commit crimes in the first place. We call that deterrence.

Third, prisons exist for the sake of retribution. That's a little strange, considering the various religious beliefs that vengeance belongs to God. Finally, we incarcerate people to rehabilitate them. Considering the high rate of recidivism, we're not very successful at rehabilitation yet.

For now, let me leave you with the story of a man named Gregory. I met him when I was a reporter working in Michigan. Greg had been a gangster. One day, he was arrested for bringing a gun to school. The judge offered this young man a choice: either finish his education or go back to jail. Greg chose school. Not only did he graduate, but he went on to college and law school.

In 1995, Greg became the youngest elected judge in Michigan state history. When we met, he told me there are four things most inmates have in common: They're young, male, black, and with no high school diploma. He said, "We can't change the first three things, but we can do something about the fourth." So, he went on to do for other young black men what was done for him.

By the way, Greg is now retired from the bench and has an eponymous, syndicated TV program. Apparently, rehabilitation is possible. Just ask Judge Greg Mathis.

87: Crime and Punishment
January 12, 2010

Today, we've been talking about various aspects of law and order, from the streets to the courtroom. It's often said that America is a nation of laws, not men -- that no man or woman is above the law. But is that true?

People make laws. People enforce laws. And despite that famous phrase emblazoned on the Supreme Court building, some people (like animals) seem to be more equal than others. Thank you, George Orwell.

There is a difference, of course, between ideals and actuality. In theory, criminals always get caught, convicted and castigated. Civil misdeeds are fairly adjudicated, innocent plaintiffs are made whole, wrongdoers are made contrite. In reality, with apologies to Dostoyevsky, crime and punishment often have nothing to do with each other.

But lest you think I'm too cynical, let me offer a dose of optimism. As bad as things are, most Americans are neither felons nor victims, neither cheaters nor cheated. The odds are you have never been arrested or sued, and you probably never will be, either.

So, why are we so concerned about law and order? Well, apart from making Dick Wolfe a wealthy man, and apart from selling all those proverbial newspapers, we must pay attention to our justice system to be sure it is there and functioning if we ever need it. Much like that tenuous health insurance policy we all want, our hope is to live as long as possible without taking advantage of it. But may your deity help you if that need does arise and there is no honest cop on the corner, no impartial judge administering blind justice, or no jury of your peers to do their civic duty.

And then, my friend, it will be too late to care.

Today, we've been talking about funding law enforcement. Crime is one of the greatest concerns in this country. Although we put a high priority on protecting the public from criminals, we often fail to put our money where our mouth is. Proposition Six fell victim to this habit. Well, I'm sorry to have to tell you this, but good police service is expensive.

Fortunately, we like law and order -- and I don't just mean the TV shows. What are there, about a hundred of them now? Anyway, we do a lot of self-policing. By contrast, I spent the past three weeks traveling overseas and was reminded of how differently others feel about following rules. One example of this is traffic regulations. While we Americans might occasionally bend the rules, most of us drive pretty well, or at least we're fairly polite most of the time.

On the other hand, in the Armenian capital city of Yerevan, drivers are a menace. Not only do they risk their own lives every time they get behind the wheel, pedestrians are in much greater danger crossing the street. Red and green lights seem to mean nothing.

At the heart of this is a lack of law enforcement. And the reason for that is corruption. To put it bluntly, cops take bribes not to do their jobs. We are very lucky here to have honest police officers. Not so elsewhere. And in those other places, traffic is the least of their problems. Corruption spreads throughout society: professors taking gifts from students, doctors getting extra payment from patients, political leaders collaborating with organized crime bosses.

Now, before we pat ourselves on the back too much, there is also a form of corruption in the United States. It's called campaign contributions. Perfectly legal, of course, but also very corrosive to the integrity of government. However limited, giving cash to public servants undermines the very notion of democracy.

Unfortunately, politicians are not likely to change a system that benefits them so much. Big commercial media companies won't give much attention to this problem either, since it profits them even more. What to do? Well, I have an idea.

Actually, it was a suggestion I first heard from one of our listeners, a regular contributor to this program. M.T. Bear proposed a law that would prohibit any non-voter from giving money to any office holder or office seeker. That would stop all corporations, unions and other such entities from buying influence. I would go even further and stop all campaign contributions. But can such changes happen? I hope we'll talk about that in future programs.

Meanwhile, I leave you with this thought: A wise man once said, "The only thing worse than breaking the law and getting caught is breaking the law and NOT getting caught. That is the surest path to anarchy."

89: Corruption in Armenia
June 2, 2009

When I first visited Armenia in 1989, it was still part of the Soviet Union. This country had just been through a devastating earthquake that left at least 25,000 dead and half a million homeless. Add to that a border war with Azerbaijan and economic collapse when the USSR fell apart. To put it mildly, life in Armenia was tough.

Flash forward twenty years. It's not the USSR anymore, but it's still a tough life for most Armenians. A tiny percentage of the population lives very well -- obscenely wealthy men and women who got their money the old-fashioned way: They stole it.

Then there is a large percentage who live in poverty, barely getting by. Finally, there's a small middle class. No wonder that many people express dissatisfaction with their political system. And yet, life goes on.

Harvard professor Marshall Goldman is a noted expert on the Soviet Union. He tells the story of a Russian peasant whose chickens were sick and dying. So, he goes to the village priest for advice. The priest tells the farmer to feed the chickens vinegar. The farmer tries it and more chickens die. The farmer goes back to the priest. The priest says, "OK, feed the chickens pepper." Now half the chickens die. The priest say, "Try feeding them castor oil." This time, they all die. The priest says, "What a pity. What a tragedy. I had so many other ideas I wanted to try."

Well, that's what's happening in Armenia. Those in charge are experimenting on the people and their country is dying.

Don't get me wrong. The Soviet Union was a dictatorship. It needed to change. But at least it provided a modicum of stability, something that seems to be lacking now. Not all change is good. As bad as the Bolsheviks were, today we see widespread corruption, human rights abuses, high unemployment and a much lower quality of life. That's a formula for drastic change, otherwise known as revolution. And as we know, that is usually a bad thing.

I leave you with this thought. When times are tough, people need a reason to hope for the future. I hope that Armenians will find that reason soon. Because as bad as things are, they can always get worse.

The most important lesson I ever learned was to listen to others. Unfortunately, that practice is far too rare in this world.

Today, we're exercising our right to choose representatives and to decide on political issues. This primary election should have been the culmination of a campaign period when we listened to facts and to honest differences of opinion. Instead, as you know, it was characterized by the ugly rhetoric that passes for public discourse these days.

I've come to appreciate the value of moderation and mediation. My hope is that these weekly radio conversations exemplify an ability to listen to each other in the pursuit of improving our Quality of Life. I'd like to take this one step further.

Beyond partisanship, our lives are surrounded by hostility. We witness family quarrels, crimes and armed combat. I understand that there will always be conflicts. But can't we come up with a better way to resolve them?

Here's my modest proposal: Let's start resolving conflicts on the air. Here's where you come in. I need to find people with disputes who are willing to talk about them publicly.

So, do you have some conflict in your life? Of course you do. It can arise from personal relationships within your family, with a friend or neighbor. It can a job-related, academic, social or political issue. It can be, in fact, about anything. The main thing is that the dispute must be real and you must be willing to try resolving your differences with an open mind, with an open heart, and in an open forum.

We'll have the help of a professional problem solvers, disinterested third parties such as today's panelists who will hear your grievances, analyze the issues, and work with both sides to find some mutually acceptable settlement.

Keep in mind that there will be no losers. Think of it as a chance to clear the air, to get something off your chest, and maybe to improve your quality of life.

It all depends on a desire for harmony. So come on, be courageous. Get in touch by phone or e-mail. Let's prove that we can make the world a better place. All we need to do is accentuate the positive.

[Note: No one volunteered to participate in such a program.]

91: Airports
March 10, 2009

Every time I fly somewhere, it makes me think about all the hassles, and long for the happier days of easy travel.

For years, I've been objecting to government agents rummaging through airline passengers' luggage, prohibiting certain quantities of liquids and gels, making us remove our shoes. Ridiculous! Investigator Richard Isaacs calls it security theater.

In my opinion, such abusive treatment is a gross violation of our constitutional protection against unreasonable search and seizure. Of course, it's much worse in the wake of September 11th. To which many Americans instinctively respond, "We were attacked. We're at war." And so on.

Well, even if you accept the premise that we are at war -- which, strictly speaking, we are not -- that fact would not give our government the right to break the law. Let me remind you that the Supreme Court invalidated Abraham Lincoln's order to violate habeas corpus during the Civil War. Imprisoning American citizens of Japanese origin during World War Two was also later ruled illegal. As was the indefinite incarceration of hundreds at Guantanamo Bay which continues even now.

As Richard Nixon finally learned, just because the President gives an order does not make it legitimate.

Today, we have a nation facing economic collapse, while still in fear of terrorism, and a new President who criticized his predecessor for disobeying the Constitution. But what has changed?

We still have American citizens subject to invasive searches at home, on the streets, and in the workplace. Not to mention what we do to non-citizens. Call me an optimist, but I'd like to live in a world where everyone's rights are respected until and unless a person is found guilty of committing a crime.

I suppose that by going along with all this, I'm part of the problem. Like most people, it's more important for me to get there than to protest. So, I just gripe about it on the radio, grit my teeth, and take off my shoes. Do you have a better idea?

92: Fire
October 13, 2009

Today, we've been talking about fire. One of the first lessons we are taught in life is, "Don't play with matches." Based on the number of negligently- and intentionally-set fires, that admonition is obviously lost on a lot of people.

While preparing for today's program, I thought about inviting someone to explain the a psychology of arson. The idea of deliberately starting a fire is totally foreign to me. Don't get me wrong: I love to watch flames. They're beautiful, fascinating. But a controlled campfire is one thing. Burning down somebody's house is quite another. And why would any sane person begin a forest fire on purpose? Of course, the answer is that no sane person would do that.

On the other hand, not all destructive fires are the result of human malfeasance. Some are simply accidents. Others are quite natural and even beneficial. Lightning ignites dry trees all the time. Clearing overgrown brush is good for the health of forests.

Every year, we spend millions of dollars putting out fires. No one would suggest that our government save money by letting everything burn, even at a time when our economy is in such bad shape.

So why is it that we argue over the cost of fighting other threats? Take medical care. Clearly, disease is a danger to public safety. Illness doesn't care whether we are rich or poor, insured or indigent, a citizen or not. So why do we make these distinctions when deciding whether to treat sick people?

I think we put ourselves at greater risk by making public policy based on such selfish, ignorance and narrow-minded views. Security seems to be of deep concern to people. What could be more important to protect than the health our of bodies? Bacteria and viruses kill more human beings than all the bullets and bombs combined. If survival is truly our main goal, let's start with the things that jeopardize it the most.

<u>93: Traffic</u>
January 15, 2008

One thing that distinguishes Americans from most other people in the world is our dedication to following the rules. The United States is often called a nation of laws, not men. From childhood, most of us are taught to value obedience over personal gain, teamwork over individual glory.

There are exceptions, of course. But as the saying goes, they are the exceptions that prove the rule.

One glaring exception to our law-abiding nature is traffic. Nearly everyone I know violates some provisions of the vehicle code quite often. They exceed the speed limit, fail to halt completely at stop signs, turn without signaling, and occasionally even drive at night without headlights. Granted, these are not in the same category with murder or armed robbery. But it is interesting to me that for a people who are so strict about law and order, we are almost universally willing to overlook some regulations rather regularly.

On the other hand, we do seem to place a high value on fairness. Bending the rules isn't quite so bad if everyone does it. We also tend to rank which laws are most important. We can overlook minor vandalism if catch an arsonist. Prosecutors can make a deal with a hit man if he'll help convict the boss. So when some drivers get stopped for going 100 miles an hour on the freeway, they say they were just keeping up with the flow of traffic. Yeah, right.

From time to time, surveys indicate what problems most affect our quality of life. This list usually includes such things as the economy, the environment, health, and security.

This is also reflected in political campaigns. Candidates used to portray themselves as being tough on crime. Today, they're tough on terrorism (whatever that means). Statistically, we're less likely to be the victims of a 9-11 type attack than to be killed by a drunk driver. So I'm much less worried about dangers in the Middle East than on the streets of Bakersfield. No one running for President promises to solve those problems. They might hunt for Osama Bin Laden, but we'll have to win the war against DUI ourselves.

Today, we've been talking about forgiveness. One of the first things I learned as a child was the value of an apology. Whether in a family squabble, a misunderstanding with friends, or something more serious, I was often taught the value of compromise. To this day, I try to admit fault or pardon others when appropriate, and to learn from mistakes when I can.

This is not to say that I am without pride. Who is? But I hope my ego doesn't get in the way too often.

On the recommendation of a listener, I recently watched a very good movie called "The Interpreter" -- directed by Sydney Pollack, and starring Nicole Kidman and Sean Penn.

Kidman's character talks about a fictional African country, Matobo. She says the people there believe that the only way to end grief is to save a life. If someone is murdered, a year of mourning ends with a ritual that they call the Drowning Man Trial. There's an all-night party beside a river. At dawn, the killer is put in a boat. He's taken out on the water and he's dropped. He's bound so that he can't swim. The family of the dead then has to make a choice. They can let him drown or they can swim out and save him. These people believe that if the family lets the killer drown, they'll have justice but spend the rest of their lives in mourning. But if they save him, if they admit that life isn't always just, that very act can take away their sorrow."

I think it's an interesting idea. I'm not sure it would work here. My experience in this country is that we tend to prefer revenge over reconciliation. I think we even prefer revenge over justice.

Think about capital punishment. According to logic and evidence, the death penalty is not a deterrent to murder. Nor does it right the wrong. No punishment can do that. And yet, we Americans are loath to follow the rest of the civilized world and ban executions.

It's the same sentiment that stands in our way when it comes to improving the quality of life. Cleaner air and water, better health care, safer roads are all achievable. But we seem to prefer holding on to the status quo, rather than make sacrifices for the future greater good. Unfortunately, in the end, selfishness does everyone the most harm.

If you agree with me, that's nice. If you don't, that's OK, too. And if I've offended you in any way, I'm sorry. Really.

KNOWLEDGE AND IGNORANCE

95: Teachers
November 2, 2005

There's a lot more going on in classrooms today than just lessons. Unfortunately, every minute that teachers must spend doing something else is time they do not spend teaching -- time their students do not spend learning -- whether it's dealing with a federally mandated test, a leaky roof or one of those pesky fire drills.

You remember fire drills: Everybody leave; line up outside single file; no running; no talking. And, of course, no child left behind.

Now, it's one thing to get everyone out of a burning building together. It's quite another to have everyone learn the same things at the same time in the same way. Some people argue that's not a good idea. Some say it's not even possible. Nevertheless, at the moment, it is the law.

There are few jobs, if any, more important to all of us than teaching. With the possible exception of parents, it is teachers who give us most of the skills and knowledge we use throughout our lives. But do we give them the respect and the compensation and the job stability they deserve? That's a question you'll be asked at the ballot box next Tuesday.

My fourth grade teacher was Mrs. Edith Robertson. One day, Mrs. Robertson reprimanded a student who said he didn't like Shakespeare. She told him, "You don't know what you like. You like what you know." Nearly 50 years later, I still remember that.

Thank you, Mrs. Robertson.

96: College
March 20, 2007

I am the first person in my immediate family to graduate from college. On one hand, that was a source of great pride for my parents and grandparents. On the other hand, it's unfortunate they didn't have the same opportunity to get a university degree, because I can only imagine how much more successful they might have been.

Of course, not everyone needs or wants to go beyond high school. Plenty of people are perfectly happy and successful without higher education. College does not make a person healthy, wealthy or wise. As I recall, that requires going to bed and getting up early -- although I'm not too sure, because I have the diploma and insomnia. But I digress.

Actually, some of the smartest people I know never finished college. They do, however, have one thing in common: a great sense of curiosity. They want to know more. I believe learning is essential for everyone, in or out of school. In my mind, that includes lots of reading. It doesn't mean only what teachers require, either. Sure, textbooks and other mandatory material are important. But so is the newspaper. So is a good novel. So is a work of non-fiction, even one with which you disagree -- maybe especially one with which you disagree.

I like to think that learning is about more than filling our minds with facts. It's also about opening our minds to possibilities. That can be done anywhere. A classroom is an excellent place to focus our energy and attention. A degree has practical value, too. Some jobs are simply unavailable without a few letters after your name.

There's one more thing about the paper chase: Occasionally, the journey determines the destination. Some people study to accomplish a goal. If you want to be a doctor, you pretty much have to go to medical school. But some people decide what to do with their lives only after they begin the educational process. Most of us don't really know what we want until we're on the way there. Some of us are still trying to figure that out.

<u>97: Literacy</u>
August 14, 2007

A few weeks ago, we mentioned that the United States ranks rather poorly when it comes to delivering medical care. The World Health Organization put us at number 37 among all nations.

Now, what about education? The federal government frequently says we're near the top with 99 percent of Americans over age 15 being literate. So, time to celebrate how smart we are, right? Well, not exactly. Literacy is the ability to read and write. But how well do we read?

According to the U-S Department of Education's own statistics, not very well. Millions of us are functionally illiterate. That means we can't read well enough to hold a well-paying job, go to college, study a voter information guide, or do any of the other important things in life that require reading.

And for those of us who are literate, what do we read? Not newspapers. The Pew Research Center finds fewer than half of us get daily news from a broadsheet, a tabloid, a magazine or even a website.

And we don't read books, either. Harry Potter notwithstanding, the book reader in America is an endangered species. According to the National Endowment for the Arts, more than half the adults in this country will not pick up a single novel this year. Poll after poll indicates that while we might not be illiterate, we are increasingly aliterate. That is, we can read but we choose not to read.

The senior book editor for the Washington Post, Ron Charles, says our reading habits are rapidly shrinking. And he blames schools in part for no longer emphasizing the classics.

But how can they? Teachers are handcuffed by dwindling resources, as well as narrow-minded and overly standardized testing. They might leave no child behind. But the children who go forward do so with less knowledge than their predecessors. Worst of all, many kids in the twenty-first century are entering adulthood without the most important skill they need: the ability to think critically.

There has never been a time when educators needed more public support than now. As much as global warming and terrorism, we risk demise from global ignorance. I can think of no greater priority than preparing tomorrow's minds today.

98: Libraries
February 12, 2008

Some people think public libraries have outlived their usefulness. Well, call me old-fashioned, but I'd rather live in a world without baseball and apple pie than give up the Dewey Decimal System.

If you're of a certain age or a regular viewer of the Sci-Fi channel, you might be familiar with an episode of the Twilight Zone. Actor Burgess Meredith plays a bookworm of a man who is always sneaking off to indulge in his favorite pastime: reading.

One day, while working at the bank, he goes into the vault during his lunch break. Suddenly, nuclear war erupts. The clerk is protected by steel walls and survives the blast. He finds himself all alone in the world. Wandering through the city, our hero comes upon the public library. Ah, it's a dream come true. Now he has all the books he wants and time at last to read.

In case you haven't seen this episode, I won't spoil the surprise ending. Suffice to say that it's a twist that would have made O. Henry proud. By the way, the first time I read that author's stories was in a library.

Say what you will about limited funds and the widespread availability of on-line information, nothing is more fundamental to democracy than the public library. It is the great equalizer. It's a center for education, stimulation and, in the truest sense of the word, recreation -- a place where we can re-create our minds.

99: Education Funding
August 5, 2008

This morning, we've been talking about state funding of public education. In this country, despite our great wealth, we do not fully fund colleges and universities. That's because we don't want to use tax dollars for anything more than is absolutely necessary. America is one of the few countries in the industrialized world where one's ability to attend college is determined in large part by personal financial resources.

Even public universities impose tuition and a variety of student fees amounting to thousands of dollars per year. And over the course of four years, attending the best private institutions of higher learning can cost as much as a modest house. By contrast, one can earn a Master's degree in, say, France for as little as $1,500.

It's no wonder, then, that many Americans do not assume their children will go to college -- not if it's a choice between education and employment. But as with most chicken and egg arguments, that is a false choice because the best jobs usually require the best training.

In her recently published book, "This Land is Their Land," author Barbara Ehrenreich writes, "a BA on your resume remains almost as essential as an e-mail address." But with no college degree, she says you can expect to earn 70 percent less than someone who has a higher education.

As a representative democracy, our citizens make important decisions. Directly or indirectly, voters set government policies. This country was founded on the word, "No." Specifically, we said "No" to British taxes. We still say "No" to taxes. Want to improve the highways? Want to provide universal health care? Want to develop alternative energy? Sorry, no new taxes. Our current president's father was famous, and then infamous for uttering those three words.

OK, fine. I get it. Whatever it is, you're against it. But then don't complain when your roads are full of potholes and your good jobs go overseas, your energy costs are determined by sheiks and speculators, or you need to use a hospital emergency room to get basic medical treatment. Too bad, buckaroo. You said, "No."

Yesterday, Gov. Schwarzenegger reportedly proposed adding a temporary one-cent sales tax to help close the state's $15 billion budget deficit. Do you want to educate your children? Maybe you should not just say "No."

100: Bilingualism
May 5, 2009

Today, we've been talking about one of the many things that divide us: language. It is one of the main things that make us human. It is what allows us to think and to express our thoughts and to share our knowledge and to learn and to grow.

I love language and I love languages. I know that I'm lucky to have grown up in a multi-lingual, multi-cultural, open-minded family. My ancestors came here from faraway places and adopted this country as their own. My father was the most patriotic man I ever knew. He loved America. But he never stopped loving his cultural roots. These are not mutually exclusive feelings.

You might find bilingualism to be annoying. You might consider it inconvenient to press one for English. You might oppose paying for government documents to be printed in Spanish and Chinese and a multitude of other tongues. But without these other languages, there would be no English. No entrepreneurs without French, no democracy without Greek. The list is long. If you think about it, I'll bet you can name dozens of international words you already know.

I'm an advocate for having a common language. Here, that language is English today. In fifty or a hundred years, it might be Spanish. Or Chinese. Before we get too worked up over linguistic dominance, let's remember this: The top five languages spoken worldwide -- in descending order -- are Chinese, Spanish, English, Arabic and Hindi. There are over one billion native speakers of Chinese. That is more than the other four languages combined.

I leave you with this thought: The Armenians say that for every language a person knows, he is that much more of a person. So, how many persons are you?

<u>101: Free Thinking</u>
March 3, 2009

Over the weekend, I went to see the Academy Award-winning movie, "Milk" which is about the liberal San Francisco political figure Harvey Milk. For anyone who lived in the Bay Area during the 1970s, this film will bring back some powerful memories. In case you are not familiar with his story, Harvey Milk was known as the first openly gay American politician.

He represented a significant percentage of the population who were drawn to the City by the Bay because of its reputation for diversity. But even in San Francisco there is intolerance. One example portrayed in "Milk" was a proposed law which would have banned gay teachers.

Which brings me to the theme of today's program. Many Americans view public school as a liberal institution. In the strictest sense of that word, I suppose it's true. The role of a teacher is to prepare young people to be successful and independent adults. Often, that means expanding upon what they learn at home but sometimes challenging and even contradicting what their parents believe.

And therein lies the rub. In principle, teachers and parents want what is best for kids. Each parent and each teacher can approach that goal from a different perspective. It is at the point where one does not accept the truth of the other that conflict occurs. This is particularly so with emotional subjects such as religion or sexuality.

On one side is the argument that young minds must be molded to conform to social standards and family values. On the other side is the view that young minds must be liberated -- exposed to different ideas so that youngsters can learn to think for themselves, to find their own version of the truth.

I leave you with this thought: Taking risk is essential for progress. That's why we admire pioneers. If not for those brave souls who took us into the unknown -- whether explorers or teachers -- we'd all still be living in caves.

Today, we've been discussing what we know. People often say "I know" when they really mean "I think" or "I believe." Of course, we can get lost in the semantics. But there's an important distinction between conceptual knowledge, perceived knowledge and demonstrable knowledge. For example, we can talk about the theory of electricity. We can touch a live wire and feel current. Or we can flip a switch and see the lights come on.

Similarly, when it comes to great social issues, people can debate the theory of life and death, poverty and wealth, war and peace. Or they can pass laws and impose their ideas on everyone. Such was the case with health care.

We know that universal, single-payer systems are less expensive than our free market method. Every rich country in the world except the United States offers some kind of national medical care. On average, their citizens live longer and better than we do. They go to any doctor they chose. They know in advance how much care will cost. They have no worries about personal bankruptcy due to catastrophic illness. These are not theories. They are facts. And yet, after a year of irrational debate manipulated by drug makers, private insurance companies and for-profit health care providers, we ended up with a lousy and expensive compromise.

Will it be an improvement over what we had before? Probably. Is it the best we could do? Hardly. Both Democratic and Republican members of Congress have nothing to be proud of. Neither do those who elected them. They knew what was true. And yet they believed what was false. Soon, we will all feel the consequences. I guess that's just the nature of democracy. Minority rights are supposed to be respected, but the majority gets to decide on policy. Only in this case, the majority meant those with the most money.

<u>103: Textbooks and Testing</u>
April 27, 2010

Today, we've been talking about text books and tests. It's interesting to look at the way educators develop standards and then try to apply them to all students. Why do we think everyone should or even could learn the same things in the same ways?

I've always been a follower of James Thurber who once wrote, "It's better to know some of the questions than all of the answers."

Forcing each person's brain through the same mental meat grinder denies individuality. Conformity might be convenient but I doubt that it is realistic to expect excellence or creativity when we're all taught to color within the lines, to parrot patriotic poetry, to hold any truths to be self-evident.

When it comes to political policy, we Americans love to cite the founding fathers in much the same way as we look to religious institutions for moral guidance. OK, so what did the creators of this country think about schools?

Benjamin Franklin wanted students to debate historical issues and discuss current controversies. He also thought schools should emphasize physical as well as intellectual fitness.

George Washington said public schools should teach students to value their own rights, to learn about virtue and morality.

Thomas Jefferson favored a public education system that would prepare voters to exercise wise judgment and learn to think critically.

If those are the right goals for schools, then why are we still obsessed with political correctness rather than teaching young people how to think for themselves? Of course, that's where good teachers come in. Textbooks are just tools. Despite all the standards imposed by pressure groups and politicians, real teaching takes place in the classroom.

In an era when information is easily available, wouldn't it be better for students to learn what good news reporters do: Find accurate facts, evaluate credibility, communicate clearly and honestly. Call me biased, but I believe we could all benefit from a little basic journalism. That's as simple as A-B-C.

<u>104: Summer School</u>
July 6, 2010

One of the things people still admire about this country is its education system. Granted, our schools face enormous challenges today. But we do have a lot of choices and a vast potential for learning. Every year, thousands of people come to the United States just to acquire knowledge.

Speaking of which, you've undoubtedly heard recent reports about the arrest of some alleged Russian spies. Who would have thought that a generation after the Soviet Union unraveled, we'd still be worried about secret agents? But as an old KGB man once told me, we'll always need spies. Americans are notoriously bad at espionage. I think that's because secrecy goes against our cultural nature. We thrive on openness. In Poor Richard's Almanac, Benjamin Franklin wrote: "Three may keep a secret if two of them are dead."

The free exchange of information is fundamental to our way of life. No wonder, then, that we hate lying. Oh, we do lie. We're just not very good at it. And spies lie. News reporters overseas are often suspected of espionage. And when you think about it, there's not much difference between how a foreign correspondent works and what a spy does. One is sent to snoop around in other countries, collect information through any means necessary, and use sophisticated electronic devices to transmit data, while avoiding government countermeasures. The other is a spy.

And what does all this have to do with summer school? It's all about information. Wouldn't you think that with all the resources at our disposal, we'd be learning more. And yet, we tell young people to put their brains on hold from June to August. What's the reason for this educational hiatus? Ours is no longer an economy that depend largely on small family farms. Even in the Central Valley, relatively few children are needed to handle the harvest. So why not have year-round school? Before you say that we can't afford it, think about what it costs us not to do it. And think about the long-term consequences of cutting education budgets, hiring fewer teachers, buying fewer books.

Lengthy summer vacations lead to graduating students less prepared than their counterparts elsewhere in the world who spend much more time in class than ours do, and whose teachers don't have to play catch-up ever autumn. If we want to save money, I say let's keep schools open permanently. Want to have fun this summer? I say, "Go to school."

<u>105: Journalism</u>
June 19, 2006

There is a difference between what we want to know and what we need to know. Responsible news services should give us both. More than a century ago, writer Finley Peter Dunne coined the saying, "A newspaper's job is to comfort the afflicted and afflict the comfortable." I believe that requires great courage.

We should not mistake news for public relations or propaganda. Opinions are important, but merely saying that a story is "fair and balanced" doesn't necessarily make it so. Nothing can take the place of good, old-fashioned straight reporting.

On the other hand, we can not rely on only one source to be well-informed. As our population grows and changes, as our world becomes more and more complex, our need to stay up-to-date grows ever more critical. The late David Brinkley once wrote, "News is what I say it is." Well, that might have been true. But ultimately, each of us is responsible for deciding what is true, what is important, what is news. That means we must consider various sources, assorted media and many different points of view. To quote Ronald Reagan's favorite Russian proverb: *Doverat no proverat* -- trust but verify. And that's the news.

106: Disinformation
August 7, 2007

I often find myself falling into the role of media critic. And why not? It's so easy. Newspapers are shrinking, figuratively and literally. Most radio and TV news broadcasts have gone from being a headline service to something closely resembling cotton candy for the brain. It might taste good, but there's really nothing there except empty calories. And then we have the hypocrites and liars on the disinformation channel called Fox. Ah, Rupert, Rupert, Rupert. How can the same man responsible for the Simpsons also bankroll Hannity and O'Reilly? I wonder what he'll do with the new Wall Street Journal. Fair and balanced? D'oh!

At the other end of the left-right political spectrum, the local press in Berkeley criticized a colleague at the Pacifica radio station for not being radical enough. Hard core activists want a broadcaster who passes their own litmus test. It seems that these days, media extremists are doing more damage to the First Amendment than government censors could ever hope to do.

But I hesitate to complain too much. Unless we're also entertaining, curmudgeons are generally marginalized under the label, "sour grapes." As my hero Andy Rooney is mockingly quoted to say, "You know what bothers me?" Well, do you, punk?

What bothers me is that even National Public Radio is giving in to infotainment. I know, I know, you have to be entertaining to draw and keep an audience. But video vows on All Things Considered? Come ON.

Still, NPR is just about the only American broadcast news service that actually provides honest news. It's definitely the only source for in-depth international coverage. So, I guess I can put up with some fluff along the way. At least they haven't brought in someone from the Today show to anchor -- yet.

In fact, comedy can be an excellent forum for journalists. In many ways, George Carlin and Chris Rock and Wanda Sykes provide much more truth than all the "real" news presenters combined. On top of that, of course, we need a bit of laughter to help us stay sane. So, forget everything I've just said. Let's all lighten up and enjoy ourselves because it's later than we think.

April 17, 2007

When the poet Emma Lazarus wrote about those huddled masses, she certainly did not have valley fever or asthma in mind. Nevertheless, those two diseases do affect our ability to breathe free. But I want to talk about a third threat lurking in the air: hate speech, which has become a virtual cancer growing in our society.

Much of it is manifested on the airwaves. Many talk show hosts who pretend to purvey public discourse are really selling air pollution. By now, you have heard all about the Don Imus scandal. His program was far from unique. A disgusting epidemic is choking our environment. These filth mongers are flourishing. Their words are designed to inflame, not inform. They raise our ire and lower our standards. They tend to be both appalling and appealing.

So, what can we do about them? MSNBC and CBS decided to terminate one trash talker, but that still leaves myriad others. Fortunately, we are not required to listen or watch. Unfortunately, like rubberneck drivers slowing down to scrutinize highway carnage, the mere existence of such debris diminishes and inconveniences us all.

Of course, this is all very subjective. As an advocate of free speech, I certainly don't want government to tell us what we can or cannot say or show or see or hear. I want all reasonable speech to be protected. Every form of expression deserves some outlet, even content that is not family-friendly or to my personal taste. On the other hand, nobody has the right to present everything, everywhere or all the time. Some material needs special treatment. We can't always expect big media companies to put politeness ahead of profits. So the responsibility falls back on us.

I'll tell you what I have done. Using the remote control, I've programmed my TV to skip the channel position for the so-called Fox News channel which I consider to be a perversion of journalism. I would encourage you to make your own choices. Your selection of what to watch or hear is as powerful as a political vote. So, exercise your right to choose and by all means, tell others about it.

America is governed primarily by the marketplace. The lowest common denominator often dominates the landscape. But let's not lose hope. By continuing to raise the bar, we can minimize indecency. Now, if there were only a way to get rid of stupidity.

One of my favorite comedians was Johnny Carson. He used to begin many of his jokes by saying, "I've got some good news and some bad news."

A lot of people think there's too much bad news in the world. From time to time, you'll hear someone suggest that we need a newspaper or a TV station to report more good news. Supporters of the President's Iraq policy say the news media don't tell us enough of the good things our people are doing over there.

Here's the problem with that idea: News is, by definition, that which is different. As much as I would like it to be otherwise, good news is generally not news. On the other hand, there is plenty of room for criticism in the way news agencies cover controversy and tragedy.

The media deserve some of the harsh criticism in the wake of the recent tragic incident at Virginia Tech University. Everyone would agree that it was a suitable subject for print and broadcast journalists to report. But report how?

As in many similar situations, my former colleagues from coast to coast descended upon the campus like proverbial locusts. Their job was to present the facts; tell the story; inform the nation. Unfortunately, as is often true, initially there was far less information than speculation.

And why do they do it? From my point of view, it's almost a kind of professional hysteria. They seem to thrive on the worst of human behavior. I remember telling a CBS News producer on an overseas assignment some years ago that a particular military invasion had been cancelled. "Isn't that great?" I said.

"No, Terry," he told me. "Peace is bad for our business."

I conclude with a bit of good news and bad news. The bad news is that there will certainly be more bad news. But the good news is that by knowing about these tragedies, we might improve the way we handle social conflict, and perhaps prevent at least one future catastrophe.

For me, the bottom line is that news reporters must be allowed the freedom to do their jobs and work in the public interest -- not just for business interests.

December 4, 2007

America is the great consumer nation. We are the world's number one marketplace for everything from cars to carbonated drinks to creative ideas. Unfortunately, we are also the planet's leader in waste.

Consider radio. Virtually every person in the United States can listen to dozens of AM and FM stations twenty-four hours, every day. You might think that would give us a great opportunity to learn. Instead, most of the broadcast spectrum is operated (or occupied, I should say) by mediocre music, crass commercials and cheap chatter also known as "talk radio" (present company excepted, of course).

The Internet is no better. We hold in our hands and on our laps and desks a degree of processing power unimaginable to scientists just a generation ago. With nearly unlimited ability to teach, most computers instead serve our lowest appetites. Not that there's anything wrong with that, as Jerry Seinfeld would say.

According to a Neilsen Media Research study, the average U.S. home receives 104 TV channels. But typical viewers watch only 15 of those channels for ten minutes or more per week. The trend, it seems, is for us to have more choices but to exercise proportionately fewer of them.

So, are we Americans becoming stupider? Are the choices getting worse? Perhaps, as with politics, audiences are simply fragmenting into smaller and smaller segments. I offer, as exhibit A, a little thing called YouTube. If you are among the uninitiated, let me break this to you as gently as possible. YouTube and its ilk did for television what bathroom graffiti did for the printing press. It's the ultimate lowest common denominator so far. By that, I mean you can watch almost anything, but you watch it all by yourself.

So, whom are we to blame? To quote Shakespeare, "The fault, dear Brutus, is not in our stars, but in ourselves." Just as we must learn to choose carefully in a supermarket or a used car lot, it is our responsibility to be good consumers of media. There's no excuse for driving a Yugo, or inhaling even the low brand. Nor should we criticize Rupert Murdoch if we choose to watch Fox News and believe what they say.

Meanwhile, I encourage you to tell Congress not to approve the FCC plan changing media ownership rules. About one hour from now, a Senate committee will begin hearings on this plan. In my opinion, you should contact Democrat Byron Dorgan or Republican Trent Lott and let them know what you think.

110: Media Violence
March 30, 2010

Today's program has relied primarily on your telephone calls. I'm always very impressed by the questions and comments I hear from you. I particularly enjoy hearing the variety of opinions from listeners of so many different backgrounds. You're also genuinely nice, and that makes my job a lot easier.

I often hear critics say, "Journalists have a bias." And we do. Good reporters are supposed to have a bias. That bias is to be open-minded. It doesn't mean we should have no personal opinions. But our job is to seek out different points of view. It's the way we uncover facts. News agencies are not supposed to favor only one party or one policy. The mission is to present as many good ideas as we can. Unfortunately, it doesn't always work that way.

For example, there are some radio stations here in the Central Valley that broadcast programs with only one point of view. I think that's sad. Having spent time in dictatorships like the old Soviet Union, I had always believed American media to be special. The words "fair and balanced" were supposed to be more than a clever slogan.

Partisan politics has its place. But extremist broadcasters are an insult to our way of life. Like all demagogues, they pretend to have truth on their side. In practice, they viciously insult anyone who disagrees with them. That's not discourse. It's disgusting. That's not freedom. It's fascism.

Radio and TV stations are licensed by the federal government. The law says station owners must operate in the public interest. Federal law prohibits indecent programming. Now, "indecency" means material that is offensive according to current community standards. It has traditionally referred to certain body parts or bodily functions.

But maybe it's time for us to expand the definition of indecency and include lying. Maybe it's time for someone to challenge the broadcast licenses of those stations which pollute the public airwaves. If we don't put this garbage in a dumpster where it belongs, let's at least require those who sell us poison to label it as such.

Meanwhile, people of goodwill are always welcome here. All you have to do is call.

<u>111: Just Like Us</u>
January 27, 2009

Very few things bother me more than deliberate ignorance. Call me an elitist, but I don't understand why so many people have so little interest in knowledge, so little desire to know more. How can we continue to advance as a civilization -- to survive as a species -- if we are unwilling to replace fear with facts?

Over the weekend, I attended the opening of a photo exhibit in Los Angeles. The images on display were of everyday life in Iran. Never having been in that country, I was surprised by what I saw, by how much average Iranians resembled people everywhere else.

The photographer, Iason Athanasiadis, is of Greek and British origin. He spoke about the changing social and political scene in Iran. He gave us a glimpse into that population which our national news media almost never present. He humanized them. It reminded me of my own travels in Iraq prior to the first Gulf War, and how unwelcome some of my stories were, stories about the people our government wanted us to think of as enemies.

The first time I traveled to Europe, I understood how unlikely it would be for those countries to fight another war. The French and the Germans and the British are so integrated into each other's lives that it's becoming almost impossible to separate them. Any more than the United States could ever split up again. Young people I've met from Paris to Naples typically think of themselves as European, just as Californians and Floridians and New Yorkers are all Americans.

I encourage you to travel abroad. Visit some country where you think people are hostile toward us. Perhaps you'll prove them wrong, or maybe you'll discover that you are wrong, that they actually like us -- because they are just like us.

<u>112: Censorship</u>
June 22, 2010

There was a time when we learned about current affairs from newspapers. That was replaced by radio and TV. Today, the delivery system for most information is becoming or perhaps has become the Internet.

People often confuse the source of news with content. Sources are important to determine credibility. Good reporters are supposed to have multiple sources to verify facts. Skepticism is the key to reliability. Perhaps you've heard the reporter's maxim, "If your mother tells you she loves you, check it."

I have long believed that the measure of a civilized society is the freedom of its information. That includes having myriad points of view. This is why I was so troubled by the recent forced retirement of journalist Helen Thomas.

The media establishment, in lock step, condemned her for criticizing the state of Israel and its occupation of Palestine. Many people took offense at her suggestion that the "occupiers" should go "home" to Germany, Poland and the United States. They inferred a link between her casual remark and the Nazi Holocaust.

Thomas was one of the only reporters who covered the White House willing to challenge presidents and their spokespersons. She had the courage to ask inconvenient questions. Whether or not her colleagues agreed with Thomas, they should have protested the silencing of this brave commentator.

Sixty years ago, our country was in the midst of the Cold War. Anti-communist hysteria led to the silencing of many Americans who held an unpopular point of view. The U.S. senator whose name became synonymous with those personal attacks was Joseph McCarthy. One brave journalist, Edward R. Murrow, stood up to McCarthy and eventually ended his campaign of terror.

In a 1958 speech to his colleagues, Murrow talked about the importance of the news media -- particularly television -- in serving the public. I believe his words are as true today as they were more half a century ago.

RIGHT AND WRONG

113: Religion
June 26, 2006

As with politics, maybe religion is a subject best avoided in polite company. For many people, it's too sensitive to discuss at all. On the other hand, like the idiomatic elephant in the living room, religion cannot be ignored. Whether we consider ourselves believers or not, faith permeates many aspects of our lives.

More than any other people on earth, we Americans consider ourselves especially blessed. We call ourselves "one nation under God." Our money declares, "In God we trust." The song "God Bless America" is more popular than the national anthem. It's certainly easier to sing.

Having said that, do we really need to embrace any particular belief system? Even if one accepts the Divine consecration of this country, our laws guarantee freedom of religion. As the First Amendment to our Constitution so eloquently puts it, "Congress shall make no law respecting an establishment of religion."

The separation of church and state means no person should be persecuted for his or her beliefs. It also means no faith should be given preferential treatment over any other, or even over no faith at all. Now, there will probably always be some interaction between religion and politics. But fortunately, we can avoid conflicts by treating each other with respect and by using all the common sense that the Good Lord gave us.

<u>114: God</u>
August 4, 2009

Today, we've been talking about some belief systems that are less familiar than the three major monotheistic religions, at least here in America. I always find it interesting to hear people speak about the unknown. That's what draws me to journalism. It's a profession that seeks to transform ignorance into knowledge. Every day, we take a blank page and try to fill it with facts.

That's why I love this radio program so much. It gives me a chance to learn something all the time. Whether it's about politics, science, art or anything else, I am constantly reminded of how little I know. And the longer I live, the more I want to learn.

The great lawyer Clarence Darrow once said, "I do not consider it an insult, but rather a compliment to be called an agnostic. I do not pretend to know where many ignorant men are sure - that is all that agnosticism means."

One of the most difficult things for most people to admit is that they don't know something -- especially something as important as the meaning of life. Many folks simply accept traditional views and use words like God or spirit or karma. The difficulty comes in explaining those words.

From time to time, I am asked if I believe in God. My answer is always the same: What do you mean by God? I don't say this to criticize anyone's faith. I just want to understand the words we use when we talk about such important matters.

115: Respect
December 29, 2009

Today, we've been talking about a variety of holiday traditions including some different ways that people celebrate the New Year. Among other things, we make plans to improve our quality of life.

On this radio program, we talk about many of the issues and people affecting the way we live. In the process of these weekly conversations, I seek moderation in our public discourse, a far-too-rare commodity in this world.

I also encourage you to think for yourself, to respect what others think, and to express your ideas respectfully. That's a philosophy I learned from my father.

Perhaps the most important example of this today is the way we treat each other when it comes to politics. You know, public service used to be an honorable profession. Whether in law or medicine, delivering mail or paving roads, selling cars or teaching children to read, I believe those who perform all of these occupations should be treated with respect. That means paying people a living wage. It means working together to ensure proper living conditions. It means doing the right thing, not only the profitable thing.

Last week, I recommended reading or re-reading "A Christmas Carol" -- that literary classic by Charles Dickens. Here's an appropriate excerpt. Bob Cratchit says to Ebenezer Scrooge, that he always thought of Christmas as

> "a good time...a kind, forgiving, charitable, pleasant time...the only time I know of -- in the long calendar of the year -- when men and women seem by one consent to open their shut-up hearts freely and to think of people below them as if they really were fellow-passengers to the grave...and not another race of creatures bound on other journeys."

I wish we could embrace that sentiment all year long. I wish those representing us in government would behave as if we were "fellow-passengers to the grave" rather than numbers in a public opinion poll.

As for resolutions, I will do my best to follow my father's advice and treat you with respect. For now, let's prepare to ring out the old, ring in the new, and hope for the best in the year to come.

Today, we've been talking about water. This is one of those topics about which there is very little middle ground. Farmers view water restrictions as an act of war. Other consumers aren't quite as adamant, but generally prefer unlimited access to water.

By contrast, conservationists treat this natural resource as community property. Who is right? Who is wrong? This is not an academic question, particularly here in the Central Valley. Our very existence is highly dependent on what happens to our water supply. So, how should we vote on the state water bond proposition next November? It would be easy for me to keep my moderator's hat firmly in place and avoid taking a stand on this issue. But since I've made a commitment to comment, here goes nothing.

I think we need to look to the future. The availability of water today might have nothing to do with the quantity a year or a decade or a century from now. As you always hear me say, it's not only the quantity that counts. So, what about the quality of our water?

That depends on what kind of water we're talking about. Industrial water does not need to be as clean as agricultural water. Agricultural water doesn't need to be as pure as drinking water. And as you know from strolling down the beverage aisle at your local supermarket, there are all kinds of drinking water.

So, who should have the highest priority? Well, that depends on how many Californians we think will live here in a generation or two -- and how well they will live. If our economy continues to falter, we might not even afford to keep the lights on, let alone fill our swimming pools or water our lawns or grow water-intensive crops.

As with all political questions, one key argument regarding water is money. How much will it cost to get the quality and the quantity we want? Apparently, our state legislature has determined the right number to be $11 billion. The state legislative analyst's office predicts it will cost us between $600 million and $800 million per year to repay that bond. For the next thirty years. That's money we don't have for a substance we can't live without. In my humble opinion, I think we're asking the wrong question. It's not about the quantity of water. It's not even about the quality of water. It's about the quantity and quality of life.

We want and need and should have locally grown food. In a country with as much arable land as we do, it's ridiculous that we import as much food as we do. We must encourage and protect and maintain as much arable land and as many farmers as we can. But we can't do that and continue to grow as if our natural resources were infinite. And to behave as if our impact on those resources was immeasurably small. Until we come to terms with that reality, we're just dead in the water.

117: Butterflies and Flowers
May 26, 2009

Today, we've been talking about some of the many beautiful things that fill our Central Valley. Those of us who work in the news business often become obsessed with the ugly things in life. I thought it would be nice to take a little break from all that today.

From time to time, I hear people suggest that journalists report too much bad news -- as if it were our fault that history is marked by tragedy. I suppose we could spend a little less time dwelling on the dark side. Unfortunately, it turns out that most people prefer to hear about what's wrong with the world. Why else would soap operas be so staggeringly popular? Why else do so many drivers rubberneck at accident scenes? I think that's called human nature.

About fifteen years ago, I was working for CBS News in Haiti. That poor little Caribbean country was ruled by a military junta. Everyone expected American armed forces to land soon and oust the dictators. One day, I learned that there would be a peacefully negotiated settlement to the conflict. I told one of my colleagues about that development and asked him what he thought of the good news. He turned to me and said, "That's not good, Terry. Peace is bad for our business." He was only half joking.

You know the old saying, no news is good news. Reporters turn that phrase around: Good news is no news. Most of my professional travels have been in pursuit of bad news. Every now and then, I think it would be nice to search for pleasant stories. Then I come to my senses. Does that make me a cynic?

H.L. Mencken once defined a cynic as "a man who, when he smells flowers, looks around for a coffin." It's easy for journalists to be cynical. There are so many coffins. But once in a while, we should try to enjoy the blossoms without going to a funeral. Who knows? Maybe we'll even spot a butterfly or two.

This morning, we've been talking about same-sex marriage. This is one of those topics where one finds very little middle ground. Arguments usually center on morality and politics, with lots of opinions and very little enlightenment. That's why I chose to focus on the law today.

The debate over gay marriage dates back centuries. In our modern era, many countries recognize the legitimacy of same-sex couples. Homosexuality is certainly nothing new. So why do people get so upset when the subject comes up?

I guess it's a lot like the on-going discussion of health care reform. If you were to ask most folks how they feel about the underlying details, you'd probably find a lot of agreement. But put the whole thing under one big banner on the national stage and you get arguments based on ignorance, fueled by fear.

I often wish complex matters like this could be resolved outside of the political system. Rather than voting on who's right and who's wrong, wouldn't it be nice to have a small group of wise men and women to make decisions?

Yes, I know. That's not very democratic. Then again, neither is civil disobedience or filibustering. We can't create consensus with everybody yelling at each other. The best way to resolve conflict is for all of us to listen. That's what I'd like, more listening and less yelling.

Besides, I'll bet conventional and unconventional couples have more in common than they might think. Whether they're called marriages, civil unions, or BFF, that's best friends forever, newlyweds should be prepared for a lifetime of good times and bad. Regardless of your gender, here's my unsolicited advice. Try to emphasize the good times. Find the right moment to take your spouse in your arms, plant a tender kiss and then, in the words of Ralph Kramden, just say: "Baby, you're the greatest."

<u>119: Smart Presents</u>
December 12, 2008

My friend Mark Boyce was telling me that his son recently helped him solve a big problem with his home computer. It took several hours, although not nearly as much time as if Mark had tried to fix it himself. Then he told his son that he should consider this service to be a substitute for a Christmas present. The young man balked, arguing that he would have done the favor for his father anyway.

Now, I don't know whether pc repair is what most people would consider to be pc, let alone an appropriate gift for this holiday season. Then again, it was far more useful -- far more valuable -- than many other presents with a similar or even greater price tag.

And why not? Think of all the things you can do for others, services they would appreciate far beyond another gadget or knickknack. As we've heard today, there are many reputable organizations that need your support.

You can make a donation to a worthwhile cause in some else's name. And do it while they're still alive! Get someone started on a good habit by giving them rechargeable batteries. Begin teaching someone to do something useful: speak a foreign language, play a musical instrument, dance the tango.

Think of something that you'd like someone to do for you. Baby sitting for parents who need a night out. Taking a disabled neighbor grocery shopping. Planting a garden or a fruit tree in your someone's yard. Of course, be sure they want it first and that you're willing to help them rake the leaves, too.

The spirit of giving does not have to be limited to those commodities that can be purchased in a store and wrapped in a box. We've just scratched the surface of such possibilities. I'm sure you can come up with a lot of other ideas. Sometimes, the best present is simply your presence. Spend time with friends and family. Call your folks. Visit them if you can. And after dinner, offer to do the dishes.

120: Deliberate Ignorance
September 30, 2008

Some people are born with a condition that limits their cognitive abilities. Others choose not to think. Unlike mental retardation, deliberately avoiding knowledge is not excusable.

We are witnessing one of the worst periods of intentional ignorance in human history. Millions of our fellow citizens seem to be trying very hard not to know things. They also hold openly unqualified politicians in high esteem.

Meanwhile, many in government go along with this by feigning ignorance or fabricating facts or hiding what they know. In a world where we have the technological resources for most of us to find out what we need to know, it is almost obscene to close our eyes to the truth.

We are plagued by a shocking lack of knowledge. And yet, the most important questions go unasked and unanswered. For example:

- Who will decide if the so-called war on terror is ever over?
- When will we run out of petroleum and what energy source will replace it and why aren't we implementing that now?
- Would another Great Depression be worse than mortgaging the entire country for three-quarters of a trillion dollars?
- And if we do have enough money to buy the nation's bad debt, can't we also spend a small fraction of that sum to provide basic health care for everyone?

I know. These are tough questions. But let's hope the next President will be able to answer them, because this time, ignorance might not be an option.

<u>121: Who Are We?</u>
November 10, 2009

Today, we've been talking about who we are. How do we identify ourselves? Where is the line between us and them?

For many years, I tried to establish my identity by being different. I also enjoyed looking for differences in others -- differences of cultures, nationalities, accents, languages. It only took me about 50 years before I realized that we are all fundamentally the same. OK, so I'm a slow learner. These days, I find myself seeking commonality. And, of course, that's easy. We are a lot more alike than we are different.

So, who are we? It might be easier to say who we are not. Unfortunately, those who wield power usually exploit our perceived differences. How do you win in business or sports or politics without a competitor? How can you wage war without an enemy?

Some say it is unpatriotic to build bridges between people or naïve to offer a helping hand. Others argue that generosity is the key to peace and prosperity. As usual, we are ambivalent.

Most of time, we don't think about it. You and I generally just try to take care of our ourselves and our families, seeking satisfaction the best way that we can. Most of the time, there is no us and them. It's just us. I believe that's when we are at our best.

Here's my unsolicited advice: The next time someone tries to persuade you that there are monsters lurking in the dark, enemies plotting to kill you, threats to our national security, ask them to prove it. And don't just take 9-11 or the devil for an answer. Every day, people commit many more acts of kindness than hatred. On balance, people do more good -- or at the very least, benign things -- than evil ones.

So don't let anyone scare you into believing the worst of others. Remember, we all live in the same village.

<u>122: Afghanistan</u>
September 28, 2010

Today, we've been talking about the prospects for stability and peace in Afghanistan. Anyone who has studied that country knows it to be the victim of one invasion after another. From Alexander the Great to the Mongols, the English, the Soviets. American-led forces are only the most recent to visit war upon those poor people. But unlike our predecessors, the United States might actually have a chance of leaving behind something better than what we found.

Consider our history. After making all-out efforts to conquer our adversaries, the world's former battlegrounds are now flourishing. Germany and Japan are only two examples. Even our first enemy, Great Britain, is now our closest ally. Not that we should be proud of all the death and devastation preceding prosperity. But it is possible to re-build.

It's not only Americans who find a way to get rich during and after battles. A villager in Bosnia once told me that Muslims and Serbs continued to trade even at the height of their horrible hostilities. He said with a wry Yugoslav sense of humor, "We sold bullets to them and they shot them back to us."

Of course, war is not a joke. I'm also not so naïve as to think every armed dispute will have a happy ending. But I have learned that conflicts offer opportunities. I hope we will seize upon this one and continue to extend a hand of friendship after the fighting is finished.

<u>123: Reality of War</u>
January 18, 2011

Most Americans have no direct knowledge of the civil wars in Vietnam, Laos and Cambodia. Half the people alive today are not old enough to have any memories from that period. And history books alone are not enough to teach us the full impact of war -- any war.

Neither is political rhetoric. Nor the philosophies of armchair observers whose opinions are formed by theories. Unfortunately, to know the full impact of war, one must also have first-hand experience. That is something I would not wish on you or anyone else.

Let me do my best to give you some personal impressions of war. I should clarify that I was not a soldier. My observations were as a news reporter. That's not the same as being in combat. It is, however, informative to see human beings purposefully killing each other in large numbers.

Here are a few things I've learned. First, it is a solemn experience. No matter who the casualty is, one cannot escape empathizing with the death of another person.

Second, there are no winners. The only certain outcome of war is death, disability, dismemberment and destruction.

Third, there is a peculiar exhilaration in surviving such an experience. Even as a non-combatant, I got an adrenaline rush from being on a battlefield -- then, escaping with my life and body intact.

Now, every person is unique. Soldiers feel differently when fighting for their lives. But even they -- the ones I've known -- have expressed these sentiments. And the overwhelming opinion of war survivors is that it should be avoided. Please note that I do not say "avoided at all cost," because the survival of a nation often means the sacrifice of individuals.

Political leaders are only human. The decision to go to war can be a mistake. The cost of war is difficult to calculate accurately or completely. Ending a war is far more complicated than starting one.

When war becomes a routine strategy, its value (in my view) is questionable. What makes us better than those we call "enemies" when we behave as badly or as foolishly as they do? Perhaps the answer to that question is painfully obvious.

<u>124: Change</u>
January 6, 2009

We're going to hear a lot more of that word "change" this year. Over the coming weeks, we'll talk about change. But no matter what happens, some things will probably stay the same. Here's an item from the Associated Press news wire:

Dateline "Gaza City" -- An Israeli warplane attacked the home of a Palestinian leader, killing him and several members of his family including at least nine children. That story was published on July 23, 2002.

In this seemingly eternal Middle East conflict, it's easy to forget that the majority of victims are non-combatants.   Both sides target civilians. In the past ten years alone, more than a thousand Israelis have been killed. There have been more than five thousand Palestinian deaths.

The late Tip O'Neil famously said that all politics is local. So, what does war in the Holy Land have to do with us? Well, for starters, it's our money. Since 1949, we've given at least $100 billion to Israel, the largest recipient of U-S aid in the world.

We call Israel our best friend in the Middle East. One thing best friends do is tell each other the truth. The truth is that using military force against civilians is immoral. Palestinians do it. Israel does it. Hell, even we do it. But it's time to stop that behavior. We need a change.

125: Feeling Safe
March 6 2007

We Americans have an international reputation for being naïve, gullible, easily fooled. I think that's because our society was based on trust. More than in most places, we have long operated on the honor system. It's understandable.

Many of us remember a time when we could leave our doors unlocked. We knew our neighbors. Cheating was considered one of the lowest things a person could do. And calling somebody a liar was just about the worst insult imaginable. In some ways, the whole country felt like a small town.

Well, I'm afraid those days are long gone. Today, it's difficult to trust anyone. Try to use a credit card and the clerk will ask you for two forms of ID. Hiring a babysitter? You'll want to do a background check and install a hidden webcam, just to be safe. Rich people in big cities aren't the only ones who have alarms on their homes and on their cars. Even personal computers come with fingerprint readers. It's like having a Homeland Security agent right inside your laptop.

I know we want to blame it all on September 11th, but it actually has more to do with the post-Watergate era and the World Wide Web. Richard Nixon and Bill Gates taught us all to be suspicious of everyone. Too bad that's not solving the problem.

We can lock our doors and treat our fellow citizens like criminals. Meanwhile, we're giving away personal treasure while surfing the net, talking to strangers on the phone, or simply taking out the trash.

Reporters are supposed to distinguish between skepticism and cynicism. A skeptic gets at least two sources for a story. ("If your mother says that she loves you, check it.") A cynic believes nothing, no matter how many sources say it's true. Journalists are advised to be skeptical, not cynical. I think that's good advice for everyone.

Many of us understand that working for the common good serves our individual interests. Of course, it's wise to be careful. We should treat our personal intellectual property as carefully as our tangible possessions. However, we must also be careful not to go too far. Because when the trust is all gone, there'll be nothing left but locks on our doors and suspicion in our hearts. And we'll end up believing that our mothers never really love us at all.

126: Reconcilable Differences
May 4, 2010

Today, we've been talking about private enterprise and public discourse. Sometimes these basic human pursuits work in harmony, and other times at cross purposes. When they conflict, who determines which is more important?

Of course, in a free society, the answer should be that we do. Commerce and self-expression shouldn't necessarily compete with each other. We can enjoy both business and pleasure. It's all about the give and take.

Compromise is the hallmark of a civilized people. It's not always clear that we qualify as civilized people. But all kidding aside, I think we settle do our differences pretty well most of the time.

Unfortunately, it's usually the worst cases that we remember. Lifelong friends quarrel bitterly over an unintended insult. A married couple forgets the years of happiness during the days of separation and divorce. International allies go to war in spite of their greater mutual interests.

And how do we prevent differences from becoming irreconcilable? Ah, that's a question for much wiser minds than mine. But we know it can be done. Most of us manage to avoid hating our friends, our relatives, our neighbors, and even strangers. One way is by getting to know each other better, by listening to each other, by keeping an open mind.

I believe community is the key. Spending time with others, even those with whom we expect to disagree, can reduce the fears that lead to conflict. That's why town squares were always so important. That's why we need shopping malls. That's why we still need to go downtown.

127: Looking Back
January 11, 2011

January is the month named after Janus, the Roman god with two faces. One looking
backward, the other looking forward. It's a perfect time of year to talk about preserving
our past and improving our future. Today, we've been doing just that.

Perhaps the most powerful repository in human history is the collection of words and
images that comprise our media. From newspapers to broadcasts to the ubiquitous
Internet, we have a great mirror reflecting who we are and giving future generations a
way to study our species.

Unfortunately, much of what we contribute to this universal archive describes people
doing terrible things. Last weekend's news from Arizona is such an example.

The slaughter of civilians is considered heinous in every human culture and by all rules
of conduct. No one condones such acts, whether the result of personal greed or for
some political purpose. And when the killer is mentally ill as might be the case this time,
it is difficult to know how to react.

In the past few days, we've heard the predictable arguments for and against gun
control. We've heard criticism of hate speech buttressed against the defense of free
speech. What we haven't heard is an argument for changing human nature.

The use of force is inherent in all creatures. Animals fight for nutrition, for procreation,
for territorial domination. In that regard, humans are no different. The only thing that
might distinguish us is that we can choose to communicate our desires with language.
Rather than attacking each other with fists and weapons, we can limit our conflicts to
words.

In studying our tragedies, I hope we'll try to answer that most difficult of all questions:
Why? Not just, "Why do we kill?" (Although that's an important question.) But, "Why
aren't we able to prevent more violence?"

Perhaps somewhere in our growing collection of relics, some future Indiana Jones can
look for an answer. Now that's what I'd call a holy grail.

128: Final Word
February 15, 2011

On this date in the year 399 B.C., the Greek philosopher Socrates was sentenced to death. He died upholding his beliefs and speaking his mind. Throughout history, martyrs have stood up against tyranny. In recent weeks, we've seen popular uprisings topple despotic regimes in the Middle East. While it's not at all clear how those revolutions will end, the desire for liberty is palpable and universal.

Of all the freedoms we enjoy, the one I cherish most is the freedom of expression. Whether in the public square, the workplace or anywhere else, human beings should be able to say what they honestly think and how they honestly feel without causing harm. It saddens me whenever I observe people trying to prevent others from exercising this basic right.

As with all freedoms, there are reasonable limits. My rights should not interfere with yours, and vice versa. For example, my desire to say what I want must not invade your expectations of peace and quiet at home. On the other hand, my desire to hold an ignorant opinion should not stop you from telling me the truth.

Occasionally, equal rights are mutually exclusive. So, how do we balance such conflicting interests? The best way, of course, is by agreement or compromise. Failing that, we might need the help of a third party such as a mediator to help us resolve conflicts.

In rare cases, there is no clear resolution. When that happens, particularly if the law has been violated or the terms of a contract are breached, a court might decide for us. While it's generally best to settle differences amicably, no one should be bullied into accepting injustice -- whether it's a military dictator or a misguided colleague.

Agreements can be flexible. Personal integrity can not. I believe it's important to know the difference and to act accordingly.

Troubling Trend in Public Radio News
By Terry Phillips

Public broadcasters face a growing challenge: How to survive in the midst of economic troubles while preserving the fundamental standards of a free press.

Those standards include keeping a firewall between funders and the most basic decisions made in newsrooms: what stories deserve coverage and from what points of view. Unfortunately for Central Valley radio listeners, that firewall is becoming a sieve.

Financial concerns at NPR outlets across the country now play a larger role in the process of determining local news and public affairs programs. Information shows are regularly being influenced by station executives, funders and community partners.

Like all good news agencies, NPR and its affiliates subscribe to a code of ethics which says that there must be an absolute separation between journalists and sponsors. Simply put, people who give money to stations may not control content.

Traditionally, public broadcast managers deferred to journalists for our expertise. Traditionally, public radio reporters and commentators were protected from the influences of sponsors. Traditionally, public broadcasters did not base programming decisions on ratings.

Of course, journalists have always been interested in what resources our employers could provide us. Nevertheless, we continued to enjoy a healthy measure of independence from financial matters. Most importantly, we were explicitly left alone to determine what constitutes news and analysis.

The argument that owners have the right to control content because of their legal responsibilities as license holders doesn't wash. Stations regularly broadcast programs without imposing prior control. For example, NPR network news stories are neither pre-screened nor censored by local stations.

This is also true in commercial broadcasting.

When CBS sent me to cover events around the world, they trusted my judgment to tell them what the news was. That's because the reporter knows what's going on. She or he is on the scene, observing first-hand, asking questions. An executive trying to accommodate the company's commercial interests cannot be expected to make journalistic decisions.

The most important ethical standard for a journalist is trust. The reason people rely on reporters is that they can be trusted to tell the truth without an ulterior motive or a conflict of interest. That is why listeners hear such facts disclosed when an interviewee has a personal or financial relationship to the host or to the radio station.

Opinions enter into the mix, too. Last year, NPR fired commentator Juan Williams. Ostensibly, it was because he expressed opinions inappropriately. NPR reporters broadcast their opinions all the time. The network simply didn't like the viewpoints Williams held. Neither did I. But silencing unpopular views is far worse than broadcasting them.

This most recent change in public radio is the inevitable result of a business model that relies on asking individuals, corporations and charitable foundations to help pay the bills by making donations. As a longtime public broadcasting supporter myself, I've often participated in the process of going hat in hand, pleading for money. Frankly, it's embarrassing and unseemly, particularly when done so ineffectually.

Creativity today is controlled by money managers. Content now is a function of the bottom line. It's a troubling development for the once-great institution of public radio journalism.

Pass it on...

Off the Air was initially issued as an e-book. A limited number of physical copies are available by special order. If you enjoyed this book, let us know -- and please tell others about it.

Hye Books
P.O. Box 12492
Bakersfield, CA 93389

www.HyeBooks.com

Telephone: 661-835-1497
Email: editor@hyebooks.com